# Words
# on the Wall

# Words on the Wall

## *Culturizing Your Classroom For Observable Impact*

Jimmy Casas

Cale Birk

ConnectEDD Publishing
Hanover, Pennsylvania

This publication is available at discount pricing when purchased in quantity for educational purposes, promotions, or fundraisers. For inquiries and details, contact the publisher at: info@connecteddpublishing.com

Published by ConnectEDD Publishing LLC
Hanover, PA
www.connecteddpublishing.com

Cover Design: Kheila Casas

Words on the Wall. —1st ed. Paperback
ISBN 979-8-9890027-6-4

# ConnectEDD
## PUBLISHING

# Praise for *Words on the Wall*

*Words on the Wall* by Jimmy Casas and Cale Birk will undoubtedly resonate with educators committed to doing what's best for their students and colleagues! I love the authors' no-nonsense yet empathetic and practical approach to describing the steps to school transformation. It's well worth the investment for school leaders seeking to make meaningful changes in their schools.

—Jorge Valenzuela | Education Coach, Speaker, Author

In this book, Casas and Birk provide a platform for educators to dive miles below the surface of any set of *Words on the Wall*. The authors share step-by-step guidance, relatable examples, and reflective checkpoints to generate a current for you to analyze yourself and your students' purpose, power, persistence, and progress. It's exactly what you need to read to set sail and succeed!

—Andrea Bitner | ELL Teacher, Author, Mentor, Speaker

This book is a true gift to teachers and educational leaders! In *Words on the Wall*, Jimmy Casas and Cale Birk carefully examine how to create a positive school culture through the lens of collaborative leadership. Casas and Birk remind us that to see desirable behaviors in our schools, we must be living examples of the words we put on our walls. Their framework offers a supportive and scaffolded process for putting our words into action. The story we walk through provides a practical guide for teachers and educational leaders to examine their own values and craft checkpoints that lead to observable impacts. If you are looking for a road map for creating a positive classroom culture—this book, is it!

—Mary Driscoll | Professional Development Coordinator, Chester County Intermediate Unit

Jimmy Casas has done it again! Along with Cale Birk, *Words on the Wall: Culturizing Your Classroom for Observable Impact* is a combination of incredible insights, great stories, and impactful ideas to help you, your team, and your school/school district take your classroom culture to the next level. The immediate impact will benefit students and staff members alike! This will be one of the most important books you read in your career.

—Randy L. Russell, Ph.D. | Educator and Speaker,
Author of *The 3 Ships*

Jimmy Casas is a trusted voice when it comes to building and sustaining school culture. Together with Cale Birk, they bridge the gap between the dynamic realities of today's classrooms and the strategic decisions that can transform teaching and learning. If you are looking to build a culture of impact in our ever-changing classrooms, *Words on the Wall* provides an opportunity to reflect on current practices and envision a culture of care, support, and empowerment for all.

—Suzanne Dailey | Teacher, Author of *Teach Happier this
School Year: 40 Weeks of Inspiration & Reflection* and
Teach Happier podcast host

School culture is not a mistake. It takes a concentrated effort from each member of the school community. In *Words on the Wall: Culturizing Your Classroom for Observable Impact*, Casas and Birk set forth a plan of school improvement that new and experienced teachers can connect with and put into action immediately. As a classroom teacher, I appreciate the observable goals that are measurable, attainable, and relevant to the daily classroom grind. As a leader in the school building who often facilitates difficult discussions, I appreciate the real-life scenarios and conversations that come with different levels of experience and personalities. If you found value in *Culturize: Every Student. Every*

*Day. Whatever It Takes*, then *Words on the Wall* will no doubt keep you thinking and growing into an accomplished classroom teacher and school leader.

—David C. James | 7<sup>th</sup> Grade Teacher-Leader; Cabarrus County Schools, North Carolina

In *Words on the Wall*, Casas and Birk illustrate what culture looks and feels like. They take the reader on a journey with a teacher team through the book sharing observable - and doable - leadership actions. I can't wait to share this book and its relatable messages. This is a must-read for everyone; they are bringing the *Culturize* principles to life!

—Dr. Michael Lubelfeld | superintendent, author, consultant

I highly recommend *Words on the Wall: Culturizing Your Classroom for Observable Impact* by Jimmy Casas and Cale Birk for anyone looking to do the challenging work of creating a positive school culture. This book is the roadmap to making your vision a reality. The authors give you the formula by delving into the importance of co-creating a shared vision that goes beyond mere words, focusing on actionable strategies to bring the vision to life. The authors emphasize the role of collaborative leadership and collective efficacy in transforming school environments. Through real-life examples and practical tools, they illustrate how to engage all stakeholders in meaningful dialogue and joint action. This book is the perfect reminder that we ARE the Culture, and if our walk and talk don't reflect the vision and mission, then they are only words about words. This is a MUST READ for all educators who want to positively impact the lives of our most precious resource, our students!

—Dr. Tiffany Bone | Assistant Superintendent of Curriculum and Instruction, Fort Smith Public Schools

Wow! Jimmy has done it again! Joined by his co-author, Cale Birk, they share real-life stories and situations in schools that we all can relate to and grow from. Not just WORDS but observable actions that we can quantify in our students and colleagues. I love this book and will immediately put the practical and intentional strategies wrapped around the four core principles of Culturize into practice. The "press pause moments" and "Culturize Checkpoints" throughout the book make it user-friendly and allow readers time to breathe and reflect on how they can put *Words on the Wall* into action in their school community. Thank you, Jimmy and Cale!

—Andrew Marotta | Educator, author, and leader of the
    Surviving & Thriving movement

*Words on the Wall* provides a practical roadmap for moving beyond aspirational statements to create meaningful cultural change in schools. Through relatable scenarios and actionable strategies, Casas and Birk empower teachers and leaders to collaboratively build a positive learning environment where core values come alive in classrooms every day. This book is an essential guide for educators looking to bridge the gap between vision and impact in their classrooms and schools.

—Dr. Jenni Donohoo | Author and Educational Consultant

In this companion book to his bestseller, *Culturize,* Casas and Birk provide a roadmap to move good intentions from cliche to culture, from ambiguous to actual. *Words on the Wall* is a guide for embedding what's on our posters into our daily practice of ensuring learning for all students.

—Ken Williams, Author | Speaker, Disruptor, Unfold the Soul

*Words on the Wall* by Jimmy Casas and Cale Birk is the perfect expansion pack to *Culturize* your classroom. Building on the tenets from Casas's first book Culturize, readers will find inspiration, relevant examples, and strategies to operationalize culture at the classroom level. In essence, we are invited to not only talk the talk but walk the walk. And we are reminded that culture is intentional and with thoughtful checkpoints, anyone can start to culturize their classroom. A lightweight, reflective, and collaborative approach to change, this is a must-have for any change agent ready to carry the banner and be a champion for students.

—Laura Williams | 21st Century Learning Specialist

*Words on the Wall* is a must-have guide for principals and district leaders looking to transform school cultures with intention and collaboration. With practical strategies from experienced authors Jimmy Casas and Cale Birk, this book emphasizes clear expectations, shared responsibility, and actionable frameworks to create positive environments where culture is the responsibility of each of us. This book equips school leaders to bring their vision to life through purposeful actions, making it a must-have. Take the words on the wall and make them the words you live by.

—Jennifer Womble | Chief Learning Officer, Future of Education
    Technology Conference (FETC) and District Administration

School culture is the heartbeat of every successful learning community, and in *Words on the Wall*, Jimmy Casas and Cale Birk give us the tools to not just listen to that heartbeat but to strengthen it. Their stories, strategies, and examples make the lofty goal of improving school culture feel attainable and tangible. If you're ready to transform your culture, *Words on the Wall* is an invaluable resource.

—Dr. Katie Ritter | Chief Learning Officer, Forward Edge

*Words on the Wall* is such a timely book for me! Building a culture of learners and learning has been my top priority since taking over as Superintendent of my small rural district. What we were missing was a clear roadmap of sharing the HOW. We all know the why and what... it was the HOW that was missing. Words on the Wall helped me visualize the HOW with actionable steps that our team can take and share and help staff understand HOW and what it will look like or "lead to."

—Janet Avery | Superintendent, Potlatch School District

If you want to make a transformational impact in your classroom, your school, or your organization, this book is a must-read. Authors Jimmy Casas and Cale Birk have masterfully developed a powerful fusion of the *Culturize* framework and the *Observable Impact* tools to provide you with guiding principles, opportunities to reflect, and practical strategies that allow you to plan, implement, and "see" your impact.

—Michele T. Webb | District Administrator of Leadership Development, Master Facilitator and Executive Coach

Improving our school and classroom cultures so that students and teachers feel empowered to be creative, joyful, and collaborative will be the key to impacting our schools around the world. *Words on the Wall* is filled with stories of hope and the belief that someday, all teachers will walk into their classrooms knowing they have worked with their school leaders to intentionally become champions for their students, every day. This book will help to ensure that *Culturize* becomes more than a moment, but a movement.

—Salome Thomas-EL, Ed.D | Award-winning Principal, Author and Speaker

Casas's impact on schools around the globe is immeasurable. On the heels of *Culturize*, we're offered a practical and inspiring pathway to be a champion for all students as we seek to create joyful, engaging, and successful learning experiences for kids. This book by Casas and Birk will breathe life into educators at every level and every season.

—Weston Kieschnick | Educator, International Speaker, Author, Coach

*Words on the Wall* is a must-read for all educators! We all impact school culture and we all have a role to make it the best culture it can be. The resources provided throughout each chapter are skillfully crafted to provide all educators with questions, examples, and frameworks they can use to put work immediately into their current situation. Every educator will see some aspect of their school, and themselves, in this book.

—Jeff Mann | K-12 Public School Director of School Improvement

## DEDICATIONS

*From Jimmy:* This book is dedicated to my family and work colleagues who continue to love me unconditionally. Your unwavering support allows me to take on life's daily work and travel challenges with grace and gratitude. Thank you for encouraging me and supporting me so that I may continue to bring my best to the educators I serve and the profession I love.

*From Cale:* This book is dedicated to my family. To Paige and Kate, my daughters who inspire me to reach for the stars and keep me grounded as a girldad at the same time. And to my wife Lori, who keeps kids, dogs, cats, dance, volleyball, and her own incredible work together all at the same time.

# Table of Contents

∿

# Why "Words on the Wall"?

*"The culture that happens in a school is just a fluke."*

If someone said this to you as a teacher or a school leader, how would you respond? Would you agree, thinking that the culture of a school is just the luck of the draw? Or would you argue that culture is the result of a combination of great kids, caring, inclusive, and responsive teachers and support staff, and innovative, competent, and compassionate leaders?

If you are reading this book, chances are you don't think that a positive school culture is simply the result of luck and happenstance. You likely believe that while having great kids, caring, inclusive, and responsive teachers and support staff, innovative, competent, and compassionate leaders, (oh, and a supportive district would be nice as well), would be ideal, we can't just sit idly and hope for these things to come together in perfect harmony in our classrooms and our schools.

We can't just wait for all the "great" kids to show up and hope that our culture changes. First and foremost, what do we mean by "great" kids? How would we define a "great" kid? The student who sits quietly in the neatly organized classrooms in our schools? The one who just does the work? The one who makes our days a bit easier because he/she is polite, helpful, and engaged in our lessons, regardless of whether they understand the work or see the relevance to their lives? Our student population is more diverse than it has ever been, and with that diversity comes a variety of backgrounds, cultures, identities, perspectives, and dreams. Each of these contributes to the culture of our school and the "greatness" of each student who sits before us in our classrooms. Not to mention, our parents and caregivers in the school community aren't keeping the "great" kids at home; they are sending us their best and these are our students. They are members of our school community and, therefore, our culture.

We can't simply expect teachers to be caring, inclusive, and responsive either. You might be thinking "How can we *not* expect teachers to be caring?" Although you would be justified in thinking it is important for a teacher to be caring, would you agree that if we asked a group of teachers, they would all say they care deeply about kids? Yet if we asked the students of those very same teachers, they would tell us some of those teachers care about them much more than others. And when we say the words "inclusive" and "responsive," what do those words look like in practice for a teacher who is overwhelmed in their classrooms trying to meet the diverse needs of thirty students at the same time?

We also can't just hope for school leaders to be charismatic, competent, and compassionate. While it's true that a leader who possesses these three traits could help to change a culture, what if they only have one or two of these traits? What if they are incredibly charismatic and compassionate, but struggle to prioritize instructional leadership? What if they are compassionate and competent, but just can't get their message across as a leader with clarity and in a way that makes others want to follow? What if they are charismatic and competent, but fail to sincerely demonstrate that they care about all staff and students?

This book is predicated on the fact that each of us, regardless of our title, has a role to play when it comes to impacting the culture of a classroom and school in a positive way. We cannot just leave it to chance or wait for someone else to do it. Healthy cultures are cultivated when expectations are clear and everyone takes responsibility for their own behavior. Walk onto a school campus and you will see signs and banners that adorn classroom walls, hallways, and marquees. You will see staff members wearing T-shirts with catchy phrases and slogans. Consider this quote from *Recalibrate the Culture*, "As we walk the building, let's make sure that our actions reflect the words on the signs hanging on our walls so they don't lose meaning. If kindness matters, then let's show others just how much it does." (Casas, 2022, Page 31). The responsibility for ensuring the words on the wall don't lose their meaning belongs to all of us.

But as much as taking responsibility for culturizing our school is one part of the issue, there is another challenge equally difficult to navigate. When it comes to what "culture" means in a school setting, each of us likely has our own definition. Phrases that describe culture as "how we do things around here" or "what you feel when you walk into a building" are catchy but provide little direction to busy educators who truly want to change the culture in their classrooms and schools. In addition, the warmth or coolness of the welcome we get at the front desk does not necessarily reflect the climate of the entire school and those within it. If we truly want to understand and impact the culture of our organizations, we must dive deeper below the surface to see what's lurking.

In *Culturize* (2017), Casas identifies four Core principles for "culturizing" our schools. Adults in schools must:

- Champion for Students
- Expect Excellence
- Carry the Banner
- Be a Merchant of Hope

Casas helps us imagine what it takes to serve in schools that refuse to make excuses or blame students for its shortcomings behaviorally and/or academically. Instead, these schools place their focus squarely on the behavior of the adults serving there. Schools across the country have implemented programs that focus on students' behavior but, to impact student behavior to an even greater level, we must first begin by examining and making changes to the way the adults behave. At its core, *Culturize* serves as a behavior framework for educators to guide them in their journey towards excellence. Since its publication, the book has resonated with hundreds of thousands of educators and leaders around the world, not only because readers could relate to the content, but also because Casas recognizes that every staff member wants to be part of a culture in which adults fight for every student, every day, and do whatever it takes because they truly believe that together they can help every student reach their full potential.

Since the book was published, hundreds of schools have adopted Jimmy's motto of "Every Student. Every Day. Whatever It Takes." In fact, in many of the schools we have worked in over the past several years, it is common to see a copy of *Culturize* on an administrator's desk or a teacher's bookshelf. On occasion, you will see this motto painted prominently on a featured wall of the building.

Yet, when asking leaders and educators in those schools what "Every Student. Every Day. Whatever It Takes." looks like in the classroom—the types of things students would be saying, the things teachers would be doing, the types of classroom activities and assessments that show we are truly Champions for Students or Carrying the Banner or any of the other core principles of *Culturize*—we realized that schools still struggled to clarify what they would actually observe if they were truly culturizing their classrooms. Teachers and administrators knew the importance of a positive culture, and they wanted to culturize their schools. But what they also wanted was clarity on what "Every Student. Every Day. Whatever It Takes." looks like in action. Educators at these

4

schools believed that school culture did not happen by accident. They knew that culture was not a fluke, and they couldn't just wish for it to happen by simply putting the words on the wall. They needed observable actions occurring throughout the school that aligned with these words on the wall.

So what can you expect from this book? If you have seen the movie *Shawshank Redemption*, you might recall the wizened, elderly, and gentle character named Brooks. A long-term convict turned beloved prison librarian, Brooks was granted parole from his decades-long tenure at Shawshank Prison. Much to the surprise of his fellow inmates, Brooks didn't celebrate. Instead, he threatened a fellow prisoner at knifepoint in an attempt to get caught by the guards and extend his sentence. The thought of being released into a world that he perceived would be so markedly changed from the life he had become accustomed to in prison was too much for Brooks to bear. He believed that life in an institution where choices around routines, meals, and daily activities were made for him was going to be less scary than a life where he would have to determine these things on his own. For Brooks, predictability and being told what to do seemed more appealing than the unpredictability of trying to figure out what to do and having to make choices on his own.

In many ways, the situation that Brooks found himself in when he was notified of his parole is not entirely unlike what hard-working teachers and leaders face when it comes to new initiatives, approaches, or significant changes that impact their classrooms and campuses. Consider the following scenario facing one such educator:

*Connie sat there, filled with a flood of emotions. She was going to need some time to process everything she was hearing. This is not the message she was expecting to hear to close out the school year. Just last August, she had sat back and listened to a similar presentation about developing a more positive culture at the school. "Every single day I try to create a positive culture in this school," Connie thought. And we all said things were going to change this year,* but nothing ever really happened. As her principal shared the reasons why all teachers were going to be required to take a deeper look at the culture of their classrooms next year, she could feel her frustration increasing.

"We used to have a great culture here. The kids wanted to learn, the teachers all got along and did things together—but those days seem to be a distant memory. The students aren't motivated, and it seems like the tone is just not what it was before," she thought. "We tried the pep rally this year. We tried incentives for student attendance. We tried team-building activities for the staff and students. We even bought wristbands for all the kids and T-shirts for the staff, but nothing seemed to stick. And now the principal is asking us to look at our classrooms. Is she serious? Has she forgotten what it's like?"

Connie felt discouraged by her principal's comments. As the Team Leader for her grade level, she felt like the blame was being placed on her. The principal failed to mention the challenges her team had faced, including an influx of new teachers. The team had experienced consistent staff turnover the previous four years, and she had two first-year teachers on her team this year she had been asked to support and mentor. It was hard enough to change the culture of a school, never mind that our teacher teams seemed to change as quickly as our students.

Connie was now contemplating whether to say anything or to keep quiet. The last thing she wanted was to be viewed as negative, but she was unclear about what the administration was looking for and what the revised School Improvement Plan would look like in terms of developing a positive culture. In a time when accountability had never been higher, Connie was struggling to be the positive and open-minded staff member that she had been known for in her school. "If only the principal would ask for input from teachers instead of just telling us," she thought to herself. No sooner had these thoughts crossed her mind when one of her colleagues blurted out her frustrations with the principal, bringing the meeting to a close on an awkward note. "Work harder? I'm already working as hard as I can. I can't make kids want to learn who don't want to learn."

On one hand, much like Brooks and the other characters in *The Shawshank Redemption*, Connie, like many educators, at times struggled with being told to do more and what change should look like. As educators, we tend to thrive when we have the freedom to create and innovate in our classrooms to see what works for our learners in our unique context. On the other hand, when we make changes, trying to figure it out on our own can sometimes be just as daunting, especially when the concept of "extra time" tends to be more of a wish than a reality for busy teachers and leaders. So where does this leave us if we examined the words on the wall, what would those words tell us about our culture, about who and what we want to be, and the impact we are making?

We believe that empowering teachers like Connie and her team and giving them a voice to determine where they are at and where they need to go next is vital when it comes to culturizing their classrooms. The same could be said for school leaders and their buildings. Schools, teachers, support staff, leaders, and students are all moving along their own trajectory, and a one-size-fits-all approach ironically tends to fit very few and leads only to minimal short-term, technical changes. The more schools and those who work and learn within them have their "fingerprints on the sculpture" to determine the vision for the culturized classroom, to assess their current reality, to have a voice in the learning needed and the actions to be taken, the more sustainable, observable, and impactful the words on the wall will be. If we believe (and we do) that a positive school culture is the collective responsibility of everyone within the school community, then our school community needs to be part of the design, implementation, monitoring, and reflection that we do in our work to create and maintain that positive culture. In *Navigating Leadership Drift: Observable Impact on Rigorous Learning* (2023), McDowell and Birk[1] describe how "Co-" is

---

[1] McDowell, M. & Birk, C. (2023). *Navigating Leadership Drift: Observable Impact On Rigorous Learning.* FIRST Educational Resources, LLC.

our friend: leaders must co-create and co-design solutions to school challenges *with* those whom the solution will impact. When it comes to something as important as developing a positive culture (or anything we are working on in our schools for that matter), co-creation and co-design *with* educators, and the broader community are key elements to sustainable change. However, as important as co-creation and co-design are, we also know that:

1. Schools are busy places and the bandwidth available for our staff and school leaders to work on developing a positive culture is often limited by the day-to-day happenings of teaching, learning, and managing.

2. There are certain "observables," or things we can see in our students, our educators, our lessons, and our leaders, when we are truly culturizing the classroom. We must always push ourselves to move beyond the words on the wall, and if we are truly having an impact on our classrooms, we must have agreed upon observables (which we will refer to as **Culturize Checkpoints**) that describe what that impact would *look like*, and more importantly, *lead to* so we know a culturized classroom when we see it. How each school gets there will be different, and that's part of the fun.

*Words on the Wall* is written for all educators, regardless of your title, because we believe that everyone plays a critical role in shaping the culture of your organization. The same can be said when it comes to the success and lack of success for each student. No one person can lead a classroom, school, or district alone and no one should be expected to. Therefore, in each chapter, we share a story that might have us looking through the eyes of a collaborative team, a teacher, and/or a school administrator. These characters may be ones you can relate to based on situations that you may have experienced in your school. There will be an emphasis on practical research that allows us to hear the stories of people who teach, lead, and learn in schools just as we do—with kids who sound a lot like our students in classrooms that look similar to our own.

At certain points, you might also find yourself saying "Wait a minute, my school doesn't look like that" or "My collaborative team doesn't sound like that" or "I could only wish our principal did those things." If you find yourself seeing parts of chapters as idealistic, please stick with us, and try your best to add the word *yet* to your thinking. Culturizing the classroom takes persistence, and each of us is at our own place on the developmental trajectory to implement the four core principles in our classrooms. But without a clear picture of what our ideal could look like when we get there, when teams and leaders are co-creating, co-designing, co-implementing, and sharing their work to culturize the classroom, we will never move beyond the words on the wall. Hitting the target is a lot easier when we know what the target looks like, so any idyllic teams, leaders, and conversations described in the coming chapters are meant to inspire what could be.

In each chapter, we will challenge you to reframe your thinking so you begin to re-examine what you see through multiple lenses. We also aim to hone your skill sets—to develop observables for a culturized classroom, using them to assess your context, to unpack the next learning, and identify the incremental, doable steps that simultaneously push us and those around us forward. You will also see *"Press Pause Moments"* periodically throughout the book, a space for you to take a breath, gather your thoughts, and do a bit of work for yourself. Additionally, each chapter will provide suggestions and ideas that are meant to spark and ignite rather than insist.

Finally, each chapter is designed to inspire educators to move beyond the words on the wall to culturizing for observable impact.

Gandhi is often credited with the statement, "Be the change that you wish to see in the world." We wholeheartedly concur, and realize that if we truly want to be the change that we want to see, we must first be able to see the change where it matters the most: in our classrooms.

Key questions we will ask you to consider throughout this book include:

> *"If I were a student in your classroom, what would I be able to do when my teacher is Carrying the Banner for me and my classmates?"*

> *"As an educator, what would I be doing in my classroom to demonstrate to my kids that I am a Champion for Students?"*

> *"If my lessons, tasks, and assessments were demonstrating that I was a Merchant of Hope, what could they look like?"*

> *"As a leader, if I believe that culture is not a fluke, what can I do that demonstrates I am supporting teachers to implement the core principles and truly culturize our school so the behaviors of adults mirror the words on the wall?"*

*Connie was looking around at the faces of her colleagues. Their expressions mirrored what she was feeling—confusion, anger, disbelief. She thought, "Why don't administrators ever take the time to talk to the people in the classrooms about culture?" Some of the things her principal said were valid, but Connie wished her principal would ask her and her colleagues for their thoughts and ideas. Not only could the principal better understand the challenges that teachers were facing in the classroom, but teachers could also better understand the pressures faced by the principal. "If we could only work together," Connie thought, "we could figure out the culture we want to see in our classrooms and what, collectively, each of us could do to get there."*

We must be intentional in our actions and those actions must mirror the words on the wall, to ensure that we not only have a clear and observable vision, but also that we have specific goals for what the impact of the vision will look like in our classrooms. When we cultivate a positive culture that is co-designed with members of our school community by reaching out and seeking input and help from people like Connie, we will be ready to culturize our school for observable impact.

Before we jump into Chapter 1, we want to first ask you for your permission as a reader. *Words on the Wall* has been written in a way that will help you to reflect on where you are as an educator and how your school functions as a collective unit in developing a positive culture for students and adults. It has also been designed to spark, ignite, and percolate ideas of what co-creating this culture would lead to. Whether you choose to focus on the *Culturize* principles above or the values that are unique and personal to your school community, we encourage you to explore what the process could look like and the roles we must take to move ourselves forward. However, at certain times in the book you may think things such as:

+ "I'm exhausted and overwhelmed already, how can I be expected to do one more thing?"
+ "Our school needs to do this work, but how do I get my colleagues to get on board? A few of us can't do this alone."
+ "We want to do this but we don't have the leadership to move this work forward."
+ "I have tried to lead our staff in changing the culture of our school, but whatever we try seems to fizzle out after a few weeks."

At certain points in the book, you may also feel uncomfortable, skeptical, indignant, or even mad. Please know that these are natural reactions, and we are asking your permission to allow us to push your thinking, even if it leads to a bit of discomfort. Much like when we are contemplating making that New Year's resolution to begin a fitness program, we must first look in the mirror and then prepare ourselves for the fact that the first few sit-ups, push-ups, and walks around the neighborhood will make our muscles and joints a bit sore. But if we push through those first few aches and pains, we know that it gets easier and we will be better because of it in the long run.

We hope that you will permit us, through the words we share in this book, to be like the training partner who knocks on your door at 5:30 a.m. on cold, rainy mornings. The one who pushes you to do one more set, run one more lap, and reminds you to stretch even when you are in a rush to get home. We also hope the words in this book help you recognize that you are hard-working, talented, and, most importantly, human. The best fitness partners push you and also sit with you on cheat days to have a glass of wine and devour a plate of nachos because we all need to give ourselves some grace! But they are back at your door at 5:30 on Saturday morning because developing a positive culture cannot become a New Year's resolution that exists only as a fading memory in February. Culturizing our classrooms means all of us—teachers, school leaders, district leaders, everyone—coming together. No one gets a pass. And it's not for a day or a semester, but rather all the time. And it's worth it.

So with your permission, let's begin to look at how we can culturize our classrooms.

# CHAPTER 1

⌒

# Beyond Words
# on the Wall

*"Vision statements impact learning."*

At many of the workshops that we do, we ask educators and leaders their opinions on this statement. We often create a "human opinion line" with people who "strongly agree" and "agree" standing at one end, with people who "disagree" and "strongly disagree" standing at the other, with "neutral" or "not sure" at the center. We then ask individuals to stand in the spot that best represents their opinion about this statement and discuss their choice with someone in a similar spot and then with someone in a different spot on the opinion continuum. Where would you stand on this continuum? Where would you guess that most educators tend to stand?

You likely would not be surprised to learn that most tend to migrate toward the "disagree" and "strongly disagree" end of the spectrum when it comes to vision statements such as:

*"We will foster a dynamic learning classroom community where every student thrives, learns with passion, and embraces challenges through empowering educators to inspire curiosity, creativity, and lifelong success for all."*

Many of us tend to believe that vision statements themselves are made with great intentions and include powerful, aspirational words. However, words and intentions do not necessarily ensure any impact on learning. Furthermore, in many instances, the exceptions who lean toward the agree/strongly agree side tend to be school and district leaders and/or those who were involved in the creation of the vision statement in the first place.

Recently, we met with a middle school leader who was frustrated with the culture of their school. Fall break had concluded the week before and, at the last faculty meeting, the staff and the leadership team felt the school needed a "reset." Hallway behavior was getting worse, office referrals were on the rise and teachers were becoming increasingly frustrated in their classrooms. As a result, the leadership team came back to the school on the Monday following the meeting and posted their vision statement on every wall they could, made announcements each day that gave shout-outs about their vision and core values, and reminded students and staff in the hallways of it during class transitions. Some staff members also jumped on board, ensuring their classes were paying attention to the announcements and reminding students as often as possible during their lessons. Yet despite their hard work to highlight their vision and values, little had changed. In those first few days, tardies decreased and teachers reported that things were "better" in the school, but by the following week, things had reverted right back to where they were. The leader felt that bringing the vision back to the forefront didn't have the impact they had hoped, and the team and their teachers felt defeated.

Much like a school vision statement, being a Champion for Students, Expecting Excellence, Carrying the Banner, and being a

Merchant of Hope—the Core Principles of *Culturize*—are powerful, aspirational words. We would be hard-pressed to find a caregiver who wouldn't want their child to go to a school that is committed to these principles. But how might we move beyond the words on the school's marquee sign, the words on the school letterhead, the words on the staff T-shirts, and the words on the wall to impact what we can observe in the classroom?

It is difficult to know if we are having an impact on the culture of our classrooms and our school without defining what we mean by impact. Frequently, when schools examine their culture, the process starts with creating a common language around "culture," so everyone is looking through a similar lens. "What do we mean by 'culture'?" we might ask at a faculty meeting or PD Day and then brainstorm ideas around the room. This can be difficult because most of us have our own, nuanced vision of what culture means to us in our classrooms and our schools. And because of this, meetings about culture can end up in nebulous, ethereal statements filled with "eduspeak" that often leave teachers saying, "This sounds great, but what does this look like for me in my classroom?"

In *Collaborating for Observable Impact in Today's Schools* Birk and Larson (2019) define "observable impact" as "the changes in practice that can be observed in the classroom that lead to improved outcomes for students AND educators."[2] In that context, they help collaborative teams break down educational concepts into the things educators can actually SEE in their classrooms. In 2023, Birk and McDowell realized that this level of clarity for educational initiatives would benefit leaders, and extended the concept of impact observability to leadership in *Navigating Leadership Drift—Observable Impact on Rigorous Learning*[3].

---

[2] Birk, C. A. & Larson, G. L. (2019). *PLC 2.0 - Collaborating for Observable Impact in Today's Schools*. First Educational Resources.

[3] Birk, C. A. & McDowell, M. (2023). *Navigating Leadership Drift - Observable Impact on Rigorous Learning*. First Educational Resources.

But what if we applied this idea of making impact visible to something as important as culture? More specifically, rather than starting with developing a common language around culture, what if we started with developing a common language around the impact of culture? In other words, if we want the four core *Culturize* principles to have an impact in the classroom, we must start with what impact would LEAD TO and what impact looks like on our students and our educators.

Remember that "human opinion line" at the start of the chapter? Now put up that same statement, "Vision statements impact learning" but this time with a different audience—imagine doing that same exercise with students in the gymnasium. Where do we think our learners would congregate on the agree/disagree continuum when it comes to vision statements?

Stop.

This is one of those moments in the book when we can start to feel a bit uncomfortable, and that's OK. Each of us is doing what we believe is the best that we can in our classrooms. We work hard, we try harder, and we've all been there when we have spent the weekend putting our minds, heart, and soul into planning the most engaging and interactive lesson we could come up with, only to feel like we got a "meh" from our students in return on Monday. And much like vision statements or words on the wall, our lessons are the result of hard work and the best of intentions. But the truth is, we are incredibly hard on ourselves as educators. And without having clarity about what we actually want our visions, words on the wall, or lessons to LEAD TO, we often beat ourselves up by focusing on all the things we didn't see without actually noticing the things we did.

Who do we chat about in the faculty lounge? The forty students who are walking, smiling, and making their way to class in the hallway, or the two sophomore students who are wearing hats they aren't supposed to wear? The twenty-one 4th graders who did exactly what we would have hoped during the reading lesson or the three or four students who made us grit our teeth? It is in our DNA as educators to constantly strive for the perfect lesson or exemplary behavior, and if it doesn't match our thinking, we can be incredibly hard on ourselves and our students. This is why it is crucial, whether developing a positive culture or developing a lesson, to begin with what it would lead to—what we would actually observe in the classroom—to guide us on how we might get there. To maximize our impact on the culture we must see beyond the words and ask ourselves, "Are we being intentional in living out the words that adorn the signs, banners, and hallways throughout the building? Do our behaviors match our building and district values?"

> it is crucial, whether developing a positive culture or developing a lesson, to begin with what it would lead to—what we would actually observe in the classroom—to guide us on how we might get there.

Let's revisit the four Core Principles of *Culturize* shared in the introduction and explain them in more detail.

**Champion for Students:** We will never quit on a student. When a student doesn't meet your expectations, invest more time to understand their story. Show compassion and empathy. When we take time to connect to their experiences, it shows we value them and their voice.

**Expect Excellence:** We will model the behaviors we want others to emulate. What we model is what we get. We should never ask others to do what we are not willing to do ourselves. Average exists in every school, but the best schools do not allow average to become the standard.

**Carry the Banner:** We will be a positive voice at all times for our students, colleagues, and families. Do your best to create meaningful experiences for people with whom you come in contact so that when they walk away, they speak positively about their interactions with you.

**Be a Merchant of Hope:** We believe that everyone wants to be great at what they do. No student, parent, or staff member wants to be a failure. However, there will be times when people lose their way. Believe that you can inspire others to be more and do more than they ever thought possible.

Creating a behavior framework that identifies and defines the values of our organization holds us, the adults, accountable for being who we say we want to be. To do so, we must live out those principles daily, holding ourselves and one another accountable for behaviors and commitments that will lead us as a collective staff to the level of excellence that we aspire to achieve.

Before you take the next step, we will need to pause for a moment and reflect on how we are currently treating the students in our classrooms and our colleagues around the campus.

In the reflection space, and using the following diagram, take a few minutes to respond to this question: **"If I were being a Champion for Students in my classroom, what would be three things I would hope to see my students doing or demonstrating as a result?"**

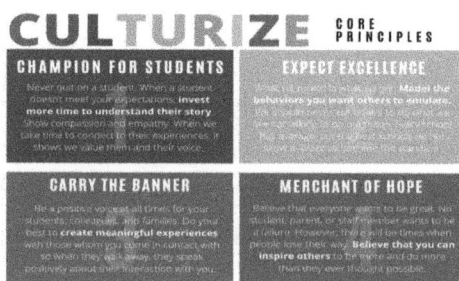

Every Student. Every Day. Whatever It Takes.

## PRESS PAUSE MOMENT: REFLECTION SPACE

♦

♦

♦

Great! You have now taken the first steps in creating your own Culturize Checkpoints.

Beginning with what we will see as a result of our work in culturizing our classrooms is a vital first step to us having an observable impact. However, there are Checkpoints, and then there are specific, descriptive, and observable Checkpoints that can be understood by anyone who reads them. As educators and leaders, we must strive for the latter.

As we described earlier, being a Champion for Students is anchored in developing a deeper understanding of the students who sit in our classrooms. It means moving beyond generalizations about "kids these days," "the entitled generation," or labeling a cohort of students as "the COVID kids." Regardless of whether we believe these things or whether there is evidence to suggest that these things are true, our students are our students. Like each one of us as educators, they, too, have their stories. Yet knowing the stories of our students is one thing, connecting that knowledge to teaching and learning is quite another. If we were to connect the content of our lessons to the characteristics of our students, what would we hope to observe from them as a result?

> knowing the stories of our students is one thing, connecting that knowledge to teaching and learning is quite another.

Look back at your list of Culturize Checkpoints that you created on the reflection page for Champion for Students. Could you see them in a classroom? Could a new teacher see them? Could someone who doesn't speak "education-ese" observe them? What about a student?

At Connie's school, her principal and the staff had come to the consensus that having teacher leaders for their teams made sense. They had tried using a model which used a rotating leadership structure, but they found that too much time was spent on trying to figure out who was fulfilling each role within the team. Furthermore, teams also appreciated the efficiency of having a single conduit to their instructional leadership team.

Connie and the staff found themselves in a much better place than they were at the conclusion of last year. Her principal, Jennifer, had stopped by to visit with her prior to Connie leaving for the summer to seek out her thoughts on the end-of-the-year faculty meeting. Although they agreed on many of the sentiments that Jennifer had communicated, they were not able to see eye-to-eye on everything. Connie did appreciate, however, her principal's willingness to listen to her concerns, specifically her feedback to Jennifer recommending she give teachers more of a voice on changes impacting the classroom.

Two weeks prior to the start of the new school year, Jennifer reached out to a few key teachers. Connie, remembering her conversation with her principal just months prior, wondered what the meeting would entail. The anxiousness that Connie felt entering the meeting was quickly dismissed as Jennifer shared how she had come to the conclusion that she needed to make some changes to her leadership, specifically in gathering more input from staff. She also shared that she realized she needed their help and that she couldn't ask her staff to make changes if she was not willing to make some much-needed changes herself.

She communicated her desire to be more intentional in working collaboratively with teachers to support them with any changes that would be forthcoming. As discouraged as Connie had felt at the end of last year, she was just as encouraged to dive back into the work with her team this year—and so was Jennifer.

Let's listen in on Connie's collaborative meeting with her middle school science team where they are discussing what being a Champion for Students might lead to in their classrooms.

*Connie: OK, each of the collaborative teams has been asked to examine culture in our classrooms. Jennifer met with the team leads and asked us to come up with three or four things we would see from our learners if each of us was being a Champion for Students in our classrooms. Each of us has read the description from Culturize, so what do we think?*

*Thomas: I think we did something like this before, didn't we? What's different this time?*

*Luisa: Jennifer really wants us to describe what we would see from our students if we were really focused on culture. I think it's a different approach—almost designing from the student and working outwards. I think we should give it a chance.*

*Thomas: Hmm. Ok.*

*Tamika: Well, if we were truly demonstrating an understanding of the stories of our students, I think they would know we care about them. (others nod)*

*Connie: Yes. I wonder what we would observe from students in a science class when they know we care about them. Any thoughts? Remember, we need to make it specific—even in kid-friendly language.*

*Luis: Maybe they would try harder for us. I try harder for people when I know they care about me. I think we would see them being resilient, and not giving up.*

*Tamika: Agreed. I would see them persevering with things that are hard and trying to solve their own problems.*

*Connie: So, we might see them making multiple attempts at solving a challenging problem, and maybe using other strategies when they aren't sure what to do next?*

*Luis: That's good. I think kids would know what we mean if we said that to them, and we could see that in science for sure. Like in labs when they aren't sure what to do next.*

*Connie: OK, one of our Culturize Checkpoints could be "Students would make multiple attempts and use multiple strategies to solve challenging problems."*

*Thomas: I can live with that.*

Connie and her science team did something very important—they went from something more subjective and difficult to see (being resilient) to something that we could actually observe students doing in the classroom—making multiple attempts and using multiple strategies to solve challenging problems.

Here are a few other examples:

**Table 1. Increasing observability**

| Harder to observe… | Easier to observe… |
|---|---|
| Doing their best work. | Doing multiple drafts that show they have used feedback. |
| Paying attention. | Able to tell us what they have heard and why it's important. |
| Being vulnerable. | Sharing stories about themselves or something important to them. |

Why is this important? For starters, each of us has our thoughts, ideas, and opinions about what things like "doing their best work" would look like. And how many of us did our best to appear as if we were "paying attention" in those first-year college classes with our eyes on the teacher, nodding, and the occasional intellectual stroke of the chin when we were thinking about upcoming Thursday night festivities with our friends? To avoid any confusion, we want to focus on what we can actually observe. Much like learning intentions, the more clarity we have about what we want to observe from our students, the more likely we are to see it in our classrooms.

Let's look back again at the Checkpoints you created. How might you increase their observability in the classroom? Ask yourself, "If I said this to a student, could they say to me, 'I'm already doing that' when actually they are not?" We lovingly call this "The Teenager Test." Here's an example:

*"Marisa, I need you to do your best work."*

*"Mrs. Travis, I AM doing my best work!"*

*"Marisa, have you done multiple drafts that demonstrate you have used the feedback that I gave you to meet more of the criteria for your essay?"*

*"Oh. Well, not yet."*

A second test we can put our Checkpoints through "The Civilian Test." For educators who have a non-educator as a friend, family member, or significant other (aka a "civilian") who is unfamiliar with your particular dialect of "education-ese," ask yourself, "Could my civilian friends observe my students doing these things in the classroom?"

A third useful lens we can look through to determine our Checkpoints is "The New Teacher Test." Would someone who has just joined our staff straight out of college be able to observe these Checkpoints if they were watching students in our classrooms?

Using the Teenager Test, the Civilian Test, and The New Teacher test, now look back at your Checkpoints for Champion for Students and:

1.  Make them as observable as possible.
2.  Prioritize them by what you would hope to observe most from your students if you were truly being a Champion for Students. Try for a minimum of three.
3.  Label them S1, S2, and S3.

## PRESS PAUSE MOMENT: REFLECTION SPACE

♦

♦

♦

Now we're moving. Perhaps you came up with a list that looks something like what Connie, Luis, Tamika, and Thomas did at their initial collaborative meeting:

| Culturize Checkpoints - When I am truly being a 'Champion for Students' in my classroom. |
| --- |
| S1. Students would be willing to share their thinking and understanding in different ways, through discussions, writing, presentations, or using technology. |
| S2. Students could explain what they are doing, why it's important, and how it connects to their lives and experiences. |
| S3. Students would explain why it's important for them to complete their work, try it multiple times even if it's hard, and use different strategies to help themselves and others be successful. |

Don't worry if your Checkpoints are not the same as these. This is that *Shawshank Redemption* moment from earlier in the book—these are examples to spark thoughts and ideas. However, the elements within these Checkpoints do provide us with evidence of being a Champion for Students in our classrooms.

If we were truly being a Champion for Students by understanding their stories, connecting to their context, empathizing with them, and valuing their voices, we should observe our students sharing their thinking and understanding in different ways. We should hear them not just complying and parroting out answers, but connecting our content to their world and what is important in their lives. And when they see meaning and realize that someone is there for them, we should expect them to want to keep trying even when it's hard.

> ## CHAMPION FOR STUDENTS - CHECKPOINT GUIDELINES
> If we are truly being a Champion for Students:
>
> + We should observe our students **sharing their thinking and understanding** in some way.
> + We should see evidence of them moving from "compliance" and parroting out answers, to **connecting our content to their world and what is important in their lives.**
> + When they see meaning in what they are doing and realize that someone is there for them, we should **expect them to want to keep trying even when it's hard.**

Have one more look at the Checkpoints you developed to see if they include evidence of the guidelines above. If they don't, see how best you might modify them to ensure that students know we have listened to them to create meaningful learning experiences that connect to their lives.

## PRESS PAUSE MOMENT: REFLECTION SPACE

+

+

+

Remember, it is not enough for us to *hope* that students will do this, or *hope* that we have the perfect student population, or *hope* we have responsive teachers and a charismatic leader. As we said earlier, culturizing is not a fluke. We must be intentional about taking steps to make these dreams a reality.

One day we were talking to a middle school teacher from the Midwest who coordinates a positive-reinforcement, points-based system to help students make good choices regarding their behavior and academic performance. She talked about the importance of clarity for students, regardless of their age:

> "It's funny. I'm not sure at what point it happens, but there is some magic age that students hit when we adults shift our beliefs from, 'We need to teach them how to do this' to 'They should already know how to do this.' It seems like this magic age is shifting to younger and younger grades, and yet we know there are adults who still need reminders and tools to help with things like responsibility, organization, time management, and positive relationships. After being in this business for so many years, I've concluded that there is no magic age at which students should already know. Providing clarity for our learners, giving them frequent reminders and useful strategies is important at any age."

Our friend makes two important points here: first, students will always need clarity, frequent reminders, teaching, and re-teaching regardless of what stage they are at in their school career. Her second point is more subtle–it's not just students who need clarity about what we would observe if we were a champion for students. Adults also need clarity about what we can do to ensure these things happen for ALL students in our classrooms. In other words, we can't wish for it

> students will always need clarity, frequent reminders, teaching, and re-teaching regardless of what stage they are at in their school career.

to happen, we must make it happen. Adopting a behavior framework for adults, as suggested in the opening chapter, helps bring clarity and allows us to determine what it is that adults must do.

This may be another one of those uncomfortable moments for us while reading this book. No doubt asking teachers to do one more thing is about as popular as when someone forgets to bring food to the staff meeting or the copy machine is left jammed by the last user. However, we are asking you to stick with us at this point, and hear us out. Like the training partner we mentioned earlier, this is us saying we understand that most people don't like to stretch and do sit-ups: not only does it take time, but it also hurts a bit, too. But by connecting our actions to what we hope to see from all our students, not only can we begin to see that our Culturize Checkpoints have an impact, but we can also begin to build our efficacy through feeling that (like stretching and sit-ups) our work to culturize our classrooms makes a difference where it matters to us the most. Let's rejoin Connie and the rest of her team as they continue to envision their Culturize Checkpoints:

> Connie: I think we got off to a good start at our last collaborative meeting. When I brought the Culturize Checkpoints we made last time to the team leader meeting, a number of the other team leaders had similar Checkpoints from their teams. It's good to know that we are on the same page.
>
> Thomas: I think many of us know that culture is an issue at the school, so that's not too surprising.
>
> Luis: I also think that demonstrates that our staff has a common set of beliefs around what is best for the kids. That's exciting to me. I don't think we've really had a common set of anything at the school for a long time.

*Tamika: I thought Jennifer's point at the last staff meeting about our failed behavior matrix from last year was really interesting. She said, "We made a behavior matrix for students, but we didn't make one for us as adults."*

*Thomas: Teachers know how to behave.*

*Tamika: Yes, maybe, but we don't necessarily know how to get all our students to demonstrate those things we want to see in the classroom. As she said, the behavior matrix became more of an adult "wish list."*

*Connie: That's our goal today—to begin to consider specific things we could do as educators to make these things happen more often for all our students. Jennifer asked us to consider one thing we could do for each one of our Checkpoints.*

*Luis: Cool, let's try the first one: "S1. Students would be willing to share their thinking and understanding in different ways, through discussions, writing, presentations, or using technology." What would we need to do in our classes to help students do this? Thomas, you're great at getting students to discuss things. What are some of the strategies you use?*

*Thomas: Honestly, I think it's because of my background in teaching English as an additional language class. With all the different languages that I had represented in my class, I realized that all the students had lots of ideas, they just couldn't communicate their thinking. So I used conferencing, portable whiteboards, and even apps—heck, anything I could get my hands on—and gave the kids lots of choices.*

*Tamika: That's brilliant—you used different ways to make their thinking visible. Wait, how do you ensure they don't always choose the same method over and over? Like, what if they just want to make Tik-Toks or draw?*

*Thomas: It was survival, but it worked. Once students were comfortable, I made "decreasing choice boards," where they got to choose a method but only a certain number of times before they had to try another way.*

*Connie: Ahh, that makes sense. Luis, your kids are always sharing things in your class—what do you do?*

*Luis: I try to spend a lot of time getting to know their backgrounds—I do identity projects and individual student interviews at the start of each term, and then I try to ensure that each unit has some little piece of them in it. I also do my own identity project so they get to know me and my family. I think they like my dog better than they like me!*

*Connie: Well, that sounds like a good start: "educators would use a variety of methods to give students choices in how they show their thinking." And it seems like we might want to include something about formative assessment as well.*

The team is making great progress in creating observable Checkpoints for students and for themselves. When making Checkpoints, we often begin with "How…?" questions, such as, "How do we get all our students to….?" Sometimes when we want to inspire new thinking, we can also push ourselves with "When…?" questions. For example, if we wanted to spark some ideas for our team when considering this Culturize Checkpoint:

*S3. Students would explain why it's important for them to complete their work, try it multiple times even if it's hard, and use different strategies to help themselves and others be successful.*

rather than asking ourselves "How do we do this?", we might ask "*When we have seen students wanting to do this, what did we notice?*" or "*When would students want to try something multiple times, even when it's hard?*" These questions move us to reflect on successes we've seen in the past and/or help us to identify with our learners and understand a learner's perspective.

For example, when considering S3, students *will* try things multiple times—when it is important to them. Students *will* try multiple strategies to solve a problem—when they need to solve the problem (watch how resourceful they become if a social media app isn't working properly on their phone). They *will* help their peers to be successful—when they feel connected to their peers and know their peers' stories. When culturizing the classroom, it's our work to connect our content to things that are important to them. It's our work to create problems that they need to solve and to develop a culture in our classrooms in which students know each other and feel connections to other members of the classroom.

That last paragraph might feel a bit gritty, like sandpaper on our skin, to educators. Connecting with students can be difficult at times. Getting to know their stories can also be challenging, rewarding, enlightening, and heartbreaking all in the same moment. Finding ways to make math and mythology meaningful to an eleven-year-old—who seems more connected to their phone than to the classroom—can be daunting. However, the goal of creating Culturize Checkpoints for educators is not to make us feel bad; rather, it's to guide our future learning as a team and as a school. Stick with us; that part is coming later in the book, too.

In the team meeting, Tamika mentioned Principal Jennifer calling a behavior matrix for students without a behavior matrix for adults a "wish list." This is because the easy part of the behavior matrix is *making* the matrix. The hardest part is teaching each of our students to *live up to* the matrix. Much like words on the wall, the key piece to bringing a vision to life in our classrooms for educators is the HOW.

"What would it look like for us?" we ask. Much like the collaborative team's work above, this is why we must take our one-dimensional set of student Checkpoints and begin to add depth—we do this by adding a second column.

It's time to press pause again. In the reflection section below,

1. Create a second column beside your student Checkpoints S1-S3 you created earlier (HINT: leave space for additional columns).
2. For each of S1-S3 (or however many you created), try to create a corresponding E1-E3 with specific, descriptive, and observable things we would see an educator doing. PRO TIP: Remember your "tests." The Teenager Test ("But I AM resilient"), Civilian Test ("Is that jargon?"), and New Teacher Test ("So what does that look like in my classroom?") when creating your Educator Checkpoints.

| When I am truly a 'Champion for Students' in my class-room…(STUDENTS) | Students will be more likely to say each of these things when… (EDUCATORS) |
| --- | --- |
| S1. | E1. |
| S2. | E2. |
| S3. | E3. |

## PRESS PAUSE MOMENT: REFLECTION SPACE

+

+

+

By creating connections between what we want to see from students and what we can do as educators, we empower ourselves to become part of the culture-building and culture-learning process.

Here's what Connie and her collaborative team came up with–don't fret if your Checkpoints look a bit different. Creating observable Checkpoints is hard, but much like any habit, it gets easier and better with practice.

| When I am truly a Champion for Students in my classroom... (STUDENTS) | Students will be more likely to say or do each of these things when... (EDUCATORS) |
| --- | --- |
| S1. Students would be willing to share their thinking and understanding in different ways, through discussions, writing, presentations, or using technology. | E1. I use various ways to allow students a choice in how they demonstrate their understanding and thinking. |
| S2. Students could explain what they are doing, why it's important, and how it connects to their lives and experiences. | E2. I give pre-assessments and use ongoing individual conferences and formative assessments to understand what students know, their concerns, interests, and perspectives, so I can connect the learning to them. |
| S3. Students would explain why it's important for them to complete their work, try it multiple times even if it's hard, and use different strategies to help themselves and others be successful. | E3. I work with students to co-create an understanding of the importance of tasks and contexts and model different ways to solve problems. |

There are a couple of keys to their list worth noting. The first key is connection: each Checkpoint we would observe in ourselves as educators is connected to what we want to see from students. We want to make clear connections between our actions and the impact we want to see.

The second key is acknowledging that this is not an exhaustive list—undoubtedly there are more and different things we could do as educators to Champion for Students. So why did this team stick with just three? The answer is simple; because educators are busy, and we need to be realistic. Which would you think is more manageable as a teacher, a program with a long list of 30-40 strategies or a co-created list of a few things we might be able to try with our teams? Trying to do everything all at once usually leads to taking a long time to do very little. Being consistent and focused on a few things is important for teams when culturizing the classroom.

In this chapter, we wanted to provide thoughts and ideas about how a teacher or a team could take a Core Principle from *Culturize* such as being a Champion for Students and turn it into a set of Checkpoints that could be seen in the classroom. We wanted to introduce a process to ensure we started with what would actually be observed from students and then work outwards from there to help clarify agreeable practices that could be implemented by adults. We also wanted to find that balance between giving the "right" answer and allowing teams to learn through unpacking the core principles on their own, much like we unpack standards. However, it's now time to dig into the core of instruction—the tasks, activities, and assessments that further signal we are culturizing our classrooms.

# CHAPTER 2

∿

# Making Classroom Learning Irresistible

*"Furniture and 'feels' are no substitute for a great meal."*

Imagine you and a group of friends are headed out to a restaurant, hungry after a long week at work. You arrive at the restaurant and are immediately captivated by the decor: the seats and tables are comfortable and modern, the booths are private yet allow for that perfect amount of 'people watching', and the windows are so large that you can see the nearby mountains during the day and the shimmering city skyline at night. Your party is welcomed by an effervescent server who seems genuinely happy to see you, and you are promptly escorted to your table where crisp white table linens, tall wine glasses, perfectly arranged cutlery, leather-covered menus and dark wood invite you to sit down. "The feel of this place is amazing!" you say to your friends as you feel a tiny growl in your stomach. However, that feeling suddenly changes when you open the menu. You discover this restaurant offers only one entree.

To make matters worse, you are lactose-intolerant, and the dish is made from a cream sauce. You call the server to the table and tell them about your condition. He smiles and tells you not to worry, they've had lots of lactose-intolerant people eat that dish in the restaurant, and in each instance, the restaurant never heard back from those people. "You just need to try," the server assures you. You ask if they could substitute the cream with lactose-free milk, but the server furrows his brow and says he will send the chef to speak to you.

A few moments later, the chef comes to the table, speaking loudly in Italian. You attempt to explain your situation, but the chef does not understand what you are trying to say. You speak slowly, and even point to your stomach to try to communicate your message, but to no avail; the chef says something that sounds like "impossible" and walks away.

You start to get anxious. You know that when you have lactose, bad things happen to your digestive system. You say to the server "I'm starving. I want to eat, but I can't eat that entree." The server tells you to calm down, asks you to lower your voice and says, "The rest of your party seems fine with the menu; maybe you need to go to that other restaurant across the street." But you don't want to leave. Your friends are here, and you don't want to go somewhere on your own. You are now frustrated. You stand up, and knock a chair over in the process. A second, tall server quickly comes to the table and says, "It sounds like your lactose intolerance is something you should have thought of before taking this reservation. You need to leave." Which is exactly what you do, slamming the door behind you. Your friends tell you later that the server apologized to the other patrons for disturbing them, and said that, clearly, this restaurant was not suitable for you.

We should not be surprised at the anxiety and frustration you felt in this situation. You have a dietary restriction that is relatively common and you were asking for some choice, or at the very least a seemingly simple substitute of ingredients. What you got in return were messages of "Just try," "We've been doing this forever and it works," "This might not be the place for you," and "You should have managed this." It would be difficult for anyone to expect a regulated response.

An inviting decor, wonderful views, a bubbly server and a warm welcome can all add to a great restaurant experience. However, a great meal outweighs the "furniture and feels" in most restaurants. Not to mention, how many of us have that favorite hole-in-the-wall place we love to eat with rickety tables, dated artwork and sparse lighting but a chef who comes out and says something like, "I am going to cook you something special tonight because I know you love spicy food. But I remember you are lactose intolerant, so I am going to make it in a clear sauce—you will love it!"

To this point in the book, we have worked to clarify one of the Core Principles of *Culturize* by creating Culturize Checkpoints for being a Champion for Students in terms of what we might observe from our students and some different ways educators could make those student Checkpoints happen in their classrooms. However, there is another aspect that we need to consider—the activities and assessments we use in our classrooms (aka "the meal") that create the learning that signals to our students that we are truly champions for each of them in our classrooms, our "restaurants." While we do want to ensure that the learning environment is as welcoming as possible, in the end, we know it is essential our students get nutritious meals from us in our classrooms.

We also know students have different learning styles (tastes) and in some cases different "dietary restrictions" (think math intolerance or Irritable Shakespeare syndrome). If we just put the same plate of learning in front of all of our students, some will eat it because they love it (the engaged), some will eat it because they feel they have to or they want to please us (the compliant), some won't eat it (the disengaged), and some get upset and act out when forced to eat it (the disenfranchised). But these are our students, and we are the chefs. Sometimes, much like our parents might have, we need to disguise some of that nutritious learning inside activities and assessments they *want* to eat to ensure each of them has a balanced diet in our schools.

Discovering the tastes of our patrons and creating recipes they love is the true artistry of the greatest chefs and the greatest teachers in our schools; they make eating and learning irresistible. They know that they have diners of all types and recognize that when they aren't eating what we are serving, blaming them doesn't change anything. And for that matter, should we be surprised if a student who struggles with self-regulation shows their frustration with a task they struggle to comprehend? If they act out when the activity requires them to do something they have been repeatedly unsuccessful with in the past? If they storm out of the room when asked to read in front of their peers because they are too afraid to show they have yet to become a strong reader?

While there can be different reasons why students are behaving in less desirable ways that are outside of our control, our tasks, activities, and how we assess our students are elements well within our control that can directly impact how kids respond in our classrooms. It is in these moments when we as adults need to reflect on *our* behavior and *our* responses and look at our key ingredients (concepts from our content) and mix them in different ways to create activities and assessments that ensure our students don't just have an opportunity to eat but *want* to eat—and even ask for second helpings.

Dr. Richard Elmore from the Harvard Graduate School of Education said "Task predicts performance. If students are not demonstrating what we expect, we must examine the task."[4] There is much to be learned from this statement when it comes to creating a classroom where we are being Champions for Students, Expecting Excellence, Carrying the Banner, and being Merchants of Hope. The key question we must continuously ask ourselves is, "What are the tasks, activities,

---

[4] City, E., Elmore, R., Fiarman, S., & Teitel, L. (2009). *Instructional rounds in education: A network approach to improving teaching and learning.* Harvard Education Press.

and assessments we would observe that would give our students the best chance to demonstrate our Culturize Checkpoints?"

Let's consider a tangible classroom example. If we wanted students in science to "demonstrate their ability to solve problems using more than one method," which task might require students to do this at a higher frequency?

> The key question we must continuously ask ourselves is, "What are the tasks, activities, and assessments we would observe that would give our students the best chance to demonstrate our Culturize Checkpoints?"

Task 1: A science activity in which small groups of students receive a laboratory kit with each of the materials, tools, and a step-by-step protocol and lab write up template that requires them to use criteria to categorize recyclable materials as plastic, paper, cans, or waste.

Task 2: A science activity in which small groups of students are required to brainstorm, design, implement, test, reflect upon, and present different solutions to help their peers reduce garbage and waste in the cafeteria at recess and lunch.

Task 1 could lead to students demonstrating some aspects of problem-solving in taking and fulfilling roles and group dynamics or at points when following the step-by-step protocol. However, to complete Task 2, students must demonstrate the skill we hope to observe.

Please note, this does not mean that Task 1 is bad or Task 2 is good—both tasks can have value for us. But if we ask ourselves, "Which task would have the higher likelihood of leading to students demonstrating their abilities to solve problems using more than one method?"

we would likely surmise that Task 2 would have the more direct throughline to the learning we hope to see.

Task analysis is one of the most empowering things we can do as educators to culturize our classrooms. The more we use our Culturize Checkpoints (what we want to see) to guide our task and assessment design, the more we can move from merely *saying* words on the wall like:

"We do Champion for Students in our classrooms."

to describing more specific and descriptive actions we have taken to actually *be* Champions for Students and sharing what we are observing from our students as a result:

"WHEN our science team focused on being a Champion for Students in our recycling unit by <E2: having ongoing individual conferences to understand what students know about recycling, their concerns, interests, and perspectives>, THEN WE NOTICED more of our students <S2: could explain what they were doing during the recycling unit, why recycling was important to them, and how it connected to their lives and experiences>."

We see the products of our hard work, and so do our students. We would not be surprised if our students felt listened to, cared for, and valued as a result of our team constantly checking in with them, asking questions, and understanding their perspectives. In addition, cognitive task analysis, or "methods for studying and describing the reasoning, skills required, and progressions needed to master ideas that then form the basis for teaching interventions" has one of the highest correlations to increasing student achievement[5]. In other words, task analysis is just effective and impactful practice.

So how could we make task analysis part of our planning and practice using the Core Principles of *Culturize?*

Stop. Time to pause and breathe in. At this moment, you may be feeling a bit overwhelmed with the idea of looking at your lessons and units through what seems like yet another lens. You are busy. You are planning lessons with your colleagues, you're in class with your students, playing in the student/staff soccer game at lunch, chatting with parents and attending meetings after school before you sprint home to continue the ongoing course known as Life 101. We get it.

One goal of this book is not to have us do what we always do in education, which is attempting to focus on everything at the same time only to realize later that we were unable to focus on one thing at any time—never mind do it well. Instead, a goal of this book is to help us develop the habit of looking for opportunities to move away from just "words on the wall" by refining parts of our units and pieces of our lessons. Culturizing the classroom is not about being performative or striving for perfection, it's about being purposeful and persistent. Much like the pleasantly annoying fitness partner we described earlier, this book is meant to help us be what we would call "flexibly relentless" in our pursuit of becoming a model of what it means to live the four Core Principles of *Culturize* in our classrooms and our schools.

OK, breathe out. Whew.

Knowing that we are not going to do this all at once, how might we get started on answering our key question: "What are the tasks and assessments we would observe that would give our students the best chance to demonstrate our Culturize Checkpoints?"

---

[5] Visible Learning MetaX (2023). Visible Learning. https://www.visiblelearning metax.com/influences/view/cognitive_task_analysis

While it may sound odd, sometimes when we envision tasks and assessments that we know would *not* lead to our Checkpoints, these non-examples can help inspire us to think of those that do. For example, if we were considering one of our observables from earlier, S1: "Students would be willing to share their thinking and understanding in different ways, through discussions, writing, presentations, or using technology" what styles of tasks and assessments could we create that would actively *discourage* students from doing this?

Let's rejoin our team to see how this might look during a collaborative meeting:

*Thomas: Creating these Checkpoints has been hard, don't we have enough already? I get the message that Jennifer is trying to send to all of us—we need to be Champions for Students, and we can't just wish for it. I know I have a role to play in this as a teacher. Why can't we just move on?*

*Luis: Actually, I need some help with this. I have a better understanding of what we want to see from our students and some things we can do as a team, but I've never really thought about what a task or an assessment would look like that truly helps our students know we are being champions for them. Can we spend a little more time on this? Between the five of us, I think we can come up with a few ideas that would really help me.*

*Thomas: That's fair.*

*Connie: Jennifer asked us to try this "creative inversion technique" as a fun way to get us thinking about 'Culturized'-tasks. We've been working on the first Core Principle, Champion for Students. Let's look at our first student Checkpoint, which was S1: "Students would be willing to share their thinking and understanding in different ways, through* discussions, writing, presentations, or using technology." What would be a task or assessment that we know would NOT lead to all our kids doing this?

*Tamika:* It would be a task where students have no choices. They would have to do it one way and one way only. (*Tamika writes this down*)

*Luis:* What about safety? I mean, wouldn't a student need to feel safe to share in front of the class?

*Connie:* Yes, so the opposite would be a task that makes students do something where they might feel less safe—talking about something they don't know, presenting in a way they have never done before, or working in groups they are not yet familiar with. (*Tamika writes this down*)

*Thomas:* I find it frustrating that students just want to Google the answer, or they just act like parrots by repeating what they've heard without thinking about it.

*Tamika:* Yes. A task where they can just copy and paste an answer—that's the opposite of what we want. Perfect! (*Tamika writes this down*)

*Luis:* I think we're getting the picture of the activities that WON'T enable students to share their thinking and understanding in different ways. Any other thoughts?

After a few more minutes of discussion, the team creates an anchor chart that looks like this to describe their non-examples:

> S1: Students would be willing to share their thinking and
> understanding in different ways, through discussions,
> writing, presentations, or using technology.

| Assessment and task non-examples | |
|---|---|
| *Tasks/assessments that only allow students to demonstrate their understanding in a single way* | |
| *Tasks/assessments based on topics that students don't know about or care about* | |
| *Tasks/assessments that make kids present their learning in using formats that are unfamiliar/ uncomfortable to them* | |
| *Tasks/assessments where students can guess, copy or Google* | |

Note that the team did not create a list of twenty different non-examples: just 3-4 are more than enough to get us started.

Now it's time for us to practice. While Connie and the team were working on non-examples for Champion for Students Checkpoint S1, we want you to try the second one. Using the table in the reflection space below on the left side of the page, take a few minutes to try to jot down three or four characteristics of non-example tasks and assessments for our Culturize Checkpoint (We included one to get you started):

S2. Students could explain what they are doing, why it's important, and how it connects to their lives and experiences.

## PRESS PAUSE MOMENT: REFLECTION SPACE

♦



♦



♦


*S2. Students could explain what they are doing, why it's important, and how it connects to their lives and experiences.*

| Assessment and task non-examples | |
|---|---|
| *Tasks/assessments that are not connected to learning and/or irrelevant to kids ("busy work")* | |
| | |
| | |
| | |
| | |

The more visible your non-examples look, the better. This helps us when we use the technique that Principal Jennifer has highlighted for her teams called "creative inversion." This is where we use this specific vision of what we don't want to observe (our non-examples) to fuel the creation of the opposite—what we do want to observe in our tasks and assessments.

Let's reconnect with Connie and her team to see how they are progressing now that they have their non-examples (listed below).

*S1: Students would be willing to share their thinking and understanding in different ways, through discussions, writing, presentations, or using technology.*

| Assessment and task non-examples | |
|---|---|
| *Tasks/assessments that only allow students to demonstrate their understanding in one way* | |
| *Tasks/assessments based on topics that students don't know about or care about* | |
| *Tasks/assessments that make kids present their learning in using formats that are unfamiliar/ uncomfortable to them* | |
| *Tasks/assessments where students can guess, copy or Google* | |

*Thomas: You know, when I look at these non-examples, I think of my own tasks and assessments. Am I doing something wrong in my lessons?*

*Tamika: I don't think this process is meant to make us feel bad; I think doing this is going to help us to see how we might tweak a few things to be more consistent in our approach to being a Champion for Students.*

*Luis: (laughs) Half of what I teach in science are things that kids don't know or care about, so I think this might be helpful.*

*Connie: Let's try this inversion process. Our first one is "Tasks and assessments that only allow students to demonstrate their understanding in one way." What would be the opposite of that?*

*Thomas: Tasks and assessments that allow students to demonstrate their understanding in different ways. (Tamika writes this down) I do that during our unit on cell function and structure. The kids get to create models and analogies to describe how the organelles work together. Do you know Evan? He did a neat presentation that related the cell to the mafia. It was really interesting.*

*Connie: Yes. I do things like that, too. But one place where I struggle with this one is during assessments—our students mostly do tests with multiple choice questions, matching diagrams and things like that. If I'm being truthful, I don't really give students a lot of choice when it comes to quizzes and tests.*

*Luis: I agree, me too. But I don't think we have to solve this right now, I think we just keep going. What about that second one, "Tasks and assessments based on topics that students don't know about or don't care about." Is it as simple as "Tasks and assessments based on topics that they DO know or DO care about?"*

*Tamika: This is where Jennifer told us to push ourselves a bit, remember? I wonder if it might be something like "Tasks and assessments that build on our students' prior knowledge and reflect their interests?"*

*Thomas: How would we do that? I guess we could use some of the stuff we get back from kids during the getting-to-know-you lessons and interest surveys we did during our first week.*

*Luis: What if they aren't interested in anything? Wait, I guess we could also look at the types of tasks—my kids LOVE competitions, or anything that allows them to create something.*

*Thomas: Absolutely. They didn't like learning about cell structure and function in the past when I had them make flashcards to help them remember, but they really enjoyed doing the models and analogies project. And, wow, did they ever do well on the test afterwards. I was surprised.*

The "push" that Tamika mentioned when making Checkpoints is key; we want to make our Checkpoints both observable and meaningful. If one of our non-examples is "Tasks/assessments where students can guess, copy, or Google," a simple opposite example would be "Tasks where students cannot guess, copy, or Google." However, we also want our examples to pass those tests we talked of earlier in the previous chapter—the teenager test, civilian test, and new teacher test. Telling a new teacher, "Make sure your tasks are ones that students cannot guess, copy, or Google," does not offer much guidance for a teacher who is just trying to survive. However, if we said, "Try giving students tasks that make them defend their thinking and apply their learning to their own context," it gives both new and experienced teachers a more specific target to shoot for in their lesson design.

Just as important as the team's dialogue about specificity is Thomas's comment about doing something wrong in his teaching. He is not. The mere fact that he and the team are beginning to reflect on the impact of their teaching on learning, specifically through the lenses of the Core Principles of *Culturize*, is the beginning of moving from words on the wall to culturizing the classroom. In *Visible Learning*, Hattie reminds us that "those teachers who are students of their own impact are the teachers who are the most influential in raising students' achievement."[6] What Thomas and the team are doing in connecting their practice to student impact is critical to the success of their students and essential for building their collective efficacy as a team.

At the collaborative meeting, Connie and the team landed on a set of Checkpoints for their tasks: some possible look-fors to describe the activities and assessments that signal we are being a champion for all students.

*S1: Students would be willing to share their thinking and understanding in different ways, through discussions, writing, presentations, or using technology.*

| Assessment and task "non-examples" | Assessment and task Examples from our 'non-examples' |
|---|---|
| *Tasks/assessments that only allow students to demonstrate their understanding in a single way* | *Tasks/assessments that allow students to show their learning in more than one way* |
| *Tasks/assessments based on topics which students have no prior knowledge or connection* | *Tasks/assessments informed by formative assessments/prior knowledge and interests* |
| *Tasks/assessments that require students to present their learning using formats that are unfamiliar/ uncomfortable to them* | *Tasks/assessments that give students choice and build their skills to present in different ways* |
| *Tasks/assessments where students can guess, copy or Google* | *Tasks/assessments that require students to defend their thinking and apply their learning to their context* |

---

[6] Hattie, J. (2008). Visible Learning: A Synthesis of Over 800 Meta-Analyses Relating to Achievement. Routledge.

When it comes to culturizing our classroom we want to get in the habit of asking ourselves that key question for each of the core principles:

*"How could I refine this task so I can be a*
*(Champion for Students)?"*

We know that a great trainer would never begin by prescribing an exercise program. Imagine if our new trainer told us that the next morning, they would begin by having us do a 10K run, followed up by a plyometric workout with burpees, pull-ups, and powerlifting. That next morning, most of us would be hitting the snooze button, because there is no one-size-fits-all approach. We want a trainer who helps us surface our goals and dreams and uses those goals and dreams to help us determine our current state and co-create the incremental steps to move us forward.

By establishing a three-dimensional (students, educators, tasks, and assessments) set of look-fors created *by* us and *for* us, we can begin to customize first steps that make sense, much like that great fitness trainer. Not a 10K and burpees, but rather the logical steps for busy educators and leaders to move forward so we can truly signal to our students "We are champions for you!"

By following a process of co-creating what our work of culturizing our classroom will lead to and using it to drive what that work will look like (much like the one laid out by Principal Jennifer, Connie, and the collaborative team) we have taken the first steps to transform the words on the wall from:

**"We are Champions for Students."**

to:

"At our school, when we are Champions for Students, you will see..."

| Our Students... | Our Educators... | Classroom Tasks/ Assessments... |
|---|---|---|
| S1. Sharing their thinking and understanding in different ways, through discussions, writing, presentations, or using technology. | E1. Using various ways to allow students a choice in how they demonstrate their understanding and thinking. | T1. That allow students to show their learning in more than one way; choice boards; digital student portfolios; presentation-based assessments. |
| S2. Telling us what they are doing, why it's important, and how it connects to their lives and experiences. | E2. Giving pre-assessments and using ongoing individual conferences and formative assessments to understand what students know, their concerns, interests, and perspectives, so I can connect the learning to them. | T2. That have varied entry points and high exit points; tasks designed with evidence of a connection to student context; assessments that require students to make a claim and support it with evidence, and a personal connection. |
| S3. Explaining why it's important for them to complete their work, try it multiple times even if it's hard, and different strategies to help themselves and others be successful. | E3. Working with students to co-create an understanding of the importance of tasks and contexts and model different ways to solve problems. | T3. Multi-step tasks connected to issues that matter to students and their community; assessments that require students to apply multiple problem-solving methods to address an issue that is relevant to their context. |

And by circling back to our three tests (the Teenager Test, the Civilian Test and the New Teacher Test) we can continue to refine our vision to ensure that our students, our educators, and our communities know what culturizing our classrooms looks like in our school.

The work of making a culturized classroom observable is challenging. In the reflection space below, take a few minutes to respond to this question:

*What are the skills and dispositions your collaborative team or your school staff would need to demonstrate to successfully create a three-dimensional, observable vision for one of the core principles (like the one above for Champion for Students)? Leave space at the top of your list for two sentences to be added later:*

## PRESS PAUSE MOMENT: REFLECTION SPACE

+

+

+

### *Skills and dispositions:*

When reflecting on the skills and dispositions needed by your team or staff to create a three-dimensional, high-resolution picture of the culturized classroom, perhaps you came up with things such as:

Collaborative

Reflective

Vulnerable

Willing to share

Empathetic

Patient

Creative

Critical Thinking

Focused

Resilient

Supportive

It's tempting to look at a list like this and think that this work of culturizing the classroom cannot be done, and that there are too many things that would need to fall into place to make this happen in our schools. And you would be right, at least in part—this can look like a lot of work. But now go back to your reflective space and add the following phrase to the top of your list:

**"Every day, I get to work in a school where our teachers and leaders are…"**

Then read your list back to yourself. If these describe the school and the culture where you want to teach, to lead, and for students to learn, then developing these skills and dispositions is important to you, and you are on the right track. Now go back to your reflective space and write one more phrase at the top of your list:

**"At our school, because of the work we do to culturize our classrooms, each of our students is learning to be…"**

If these describe the culture of a school where you would want your *own* children or loved ones to attend, then you are REALLY on the right track.

At the start of this book, we referenced Brooks from *The Shaw-shank Redemption* and the delicate balance between having things dictated by "the institution" versus the time and energy required when we have the freedom to figure things out on our own. The last two chapters have illustrated a process that a collaborative team could use to break down one of the Core Principles of *Culturize* into observable Checkpoints. You might choose to use other principles or processes that fit your context. Regardless of your school's core principles or the process that it takes to get there, there are a few essential elements in developing Checkpoints that will help schools avoid what we would call "Culturize-lite":

1. **Checkpoints need to begin with what we would observe from students.** If a core principle were happening at the highest level of proficiency and frequency, we must begin with *what we want it to lead to* for our students. These observables become the drivers of our dispositions, instruction, tasks, assessments and show us what purposeful leadership can look like in practice.
2. **The vision needs to be co-created.** This process is formative, and the development of Checkpoints is an opportunity for us to learn about each other, our values, and our diverse perspectives.
3. **We must acknowledge that we cause culture.** The way we learn about our students, the way we use that learning to inform our teaching and the tasks and assessments we design and implement in our classrooms represent the signals we send to our students about the culture that we value. Our actions lead to the culture we want to observe when culturizing our classrooms.

If we don't start with what we want to observe from students, we can fall into the trap of: "We DO culturize our classrooms. Our kids just don't get it." Our measure of success in bringing the Core Principles of *Culturize* to life in our classrooms is what we observe in our students as a result of our work. When we connect our teaching actions to the impact we can observe in our students, that culture then radiates outwards from students to teachers to leaders and the community.

If we fail to co-create the vision as a broader, diverse group, we rob ourselves of the opportunity to learn together and to learn about each other. Culturizing the classroom is not a race, it's a step-by-step process that we do together with many "press-pause" moments to reflect on where we are at, how far we have come, and where we want to go together.

And finally, we must accept the fact that we cause culture. Culture is not a fluke, and it is not one person's responsibility. It's every person's responsibility. Ask a child if their teacher likes them. Ask if their teacher takes the time to understand how they learn best. Find out if they are given the means and opportunities to show what they know. See if they feel their teacher thinks they are capable. Students can judge these things at a very young age, and the signals we give through our approaches to our students, teaching, and activities are their evidence. Now ask teachers the same questions about their administration and principals about their superintendent. We *all* cause culture.

> we must accept the fact that we cause culture. Culture is not a fluke, and it is not one person's responsibility. It's every person's responsibility.

But knowing that we cause culture is also an incredible opportunity—we can make a difference. It is empowering to know that we can create a set of Checkpoints made by us and for us that are doable make a difference.

In the next chapters, we want to expand our view of the school as a whole. We want to suggest ideas that schools can use to get more

55

"fingerprints on the sculpture" in co-creating the vision for each of the Core Principles. While you will find a sample set of Checkpoints for each of the Core Principles in the Appendix to give you thoughts and ideas, we strongly encourage you to see the examples as reference points rather than right answers. The right answer is developing these Checkpoints with colleagues at your own school.

We also want to help schools go deeper with their Checkpoints, using them to determine where they are at currently and what learning makes sense going forward. To use their Checkpoints as tools to help refine lessons, inspire staff meetings that model core principles, and create immersive professional learning experiences that help design, implement, reflect upon, and share our collective work to culturize our classrooms.

Our goal is to help schools work together to move from culturizing *one* classroom to culturizing *all* classrooms. This doesn't happen by accident, nor can we just wish for this to happen.

It's time for us to talk about the role that, to this point, we have left sitting on the sidelines. Let's press pause and spend some time talking a bit about the role of the administrator, Principal Jennifer.

## PRESS PAUSE MOMENT: REFLECTION SPACE

# CHAPTER 3

+

+

+

~

# Leadership is Not a Spectator Sport

*"We are continually faced with great opportunities*
*which are brilliantly disguised as unsolvable problems."*

—Margaret Mead

In 2007, Viviane Robinson wrote a research paper called "The Impact of Leadership on Student Outcomes: Making Sense of the Evidence." Within her research, she investigated five sets of leadership practices and their impact on student outcomes both inside and outside the classroom. The five sets of leadership practices were:

1. Establishing goals and expectations
2. Strategic resourcing
3. Planning, coordinating, and evaluating teaching and the curriculum
4. Promoting and participating in teacher learning and development
5. Ensuring an orderly and supportive environment

Whether you are a teacher, school or district leader, or an interested reader, take a moment to consider each of these. If you were to rank them in order of their impact on student outcomes, which leadership practice do you think this study showed as having the greatest impact on student outcomes?

It often surprises members of the school community to find that school leaders promoting and participating in teacher learning and development is the practice that leads the way. Robinson writes:

*"The more leaders focus their professional relationships, their work and their learning on the core business of teaching and learning, the greater their influence on student outcomes. It is suggested that leadership theory, research and practice needs to be more closely linked to research on effective teaching so that there is a greater focus on what leaders need to know and do to support teachers in using the pedagogical practices that raise achievement and reduce disparity.*[7]

The moral of the story in this research is that if we truly want to improve outcomes for students both inside and outside the classroom, we can't just expect it to happen nor leave the heavy lifting to teachers. The same holds for culturizing the classroom: leadership is not a spectator sport. We talked in previous chapters about the fact that culture is the responsibility of each of us. School administrators can (and must) play an active role. But given the fact that, much like teachers, school leaders are often dividing their time between lunchroom monitoring, hallway supervision, team meetings, parent concerns and car line duty, how can administrators ensure that the effort we put into moving from the words on the wall actually leads to classroom impact across the school?

---

[7] Robinson, V (2007) "The impact of leadership on student outcomes: Making sense of the evidence". https://research.acer.edu.au/research_conference_2007/5

While there are a multitude of things that administrators *might do* to culturize all classrooms, there are five things they m*ust do* to ensure that we move from words to action to impact:

1. Help us **identify where we need to go** in culturizing the classroom (co-create our desired state, aka "Checkpoints")
2. Help us **determine where we are at** in culturizing the classroom (co-assess our current state)
3. Help us take the distance between our current and desired state and **break it into manageable steps/learning/actions** to culturize the classroom (meet us where we are at)
4. **Model the practices and dispositions** required to move beyond the words on the wall (promote and participate)
5. Help us **connect our collective actions to the impact those actions have on every student** (build our efficacy through reflection, connection and sharing)

Leaders are acutely aware just how important it is to create and maintain a positive culture in our schools. This is in no small part because the responsibility for a poor culture can often be localized by the school community to school leadership. As a result, it can be tempting for a leadership team to try to fix the culture by doing a school reset to re-emphasize expectations, implementing incentive programs, creating classroom agreements, or renewing commitments to things such as growth mindset and self-regulation.

This is not to say that pieces such as these can't have a place in improving school culture; they certainly can. However, for our efforts to have an observable and sustainable impact on school culture, leaders must determine what that impact would look like and lead to in our classrooms, and how to do it WITH those who are living that culture.

*Principal Jennifer knew all about "quick fixes" for culture—she would be the first to admit that she had tried (and failed) to implement nearly every fix for the culture in her previous school that she could find or think of. The weight of school culture had felt heavy on her shoulders in her last building. As an assistant principal, teachers would frequently remind her of the rich culture and traditions that had been established over the years by the hard-working staff. When they would refer students to her office, they would remind her just as frequently of the steady erosion of that culture since the previous principal had retired. As much as she tried to, she realized that leaders could not do this work alone, and she knew she needed to do things differently at this school.*

*At her previous school, the staff would talk about "The Tiger Code," a vague characterization of lofty standards for how students should behave in the school. Jennifer and several other staff members felt that it was less of a "Code" and more a set of "carrots and sticks" that would be used to motivate or punish students who weren't complying with their teacher. When Jennifer would ask people to describe this Code so she could better support teachers and students, she would be told, "You know it when you see it, and you REALLY know it when you don't."*

*Jennifer was determined that culture would never be used as a set of carrots and sticks when she became a principal. She would ensure that everyone knew what a positive culture meant by helping determine what a positive culture would look like and lead to in classrooms, and that everyone (including herself) would be engaged in the process by fulfilling roles to make culture come to life in each classroom of the school.*

When it comes to culturizing the classroom, school leadership plays a significant role. In the space below, take a few moments to reflect on the characteristics and attributes that you feel are critical in supporting teachers to culturize their classrooms.

## PRESS PAUSE MOMENT: REFLECTION SPACE

The characteristics and attributes of a school leader who supports each teacher in culturizing the classroom include:

+

+

+

Perhaps you listed attributes such as: flexible, relationship-centered, and collaborative. Or: focused, supportive, and empathetic. Or others that we have researched or experienced in our lives and careers that we felt were particularly effective in moving us from where we were at to where we needed to go in our school. You would be correct: each of these would be important to help us rekindle the culture of our school.

Unfortunately, creating the vision for this culture-transforming leader can be as challenging and nebulous as defining culture itself. For educators, no matter how hard we try, we end up making a "Franken-leader," a collection of idealistic traits we have gathered from our educational travels, bolted together to form something which amounts to wishful thinking and prevents us from getting started because we know that we will never have that perfect leader in our context. Or worse, our vision doesn't pass the Teenager Test when we have a leader who professes to be flexible, supportive, and empathetic, but fails to back those claims up with the requisite actions.

But don't despair; here's the good news: By having her staff begin to co-create what a culturized classroom would look like in terms of students, staff, and tasks, Principal Jennifer did two things:

1. She helped her staff make their thinking, values, and beliefs about school culture observable so she could begin to plan the next steps to meet them where they were at.
2. She created a set of Checkpoints that would let her know if her leadership was having an impact on the culture of the school.

Co-creating observable Checkpoints to culturize our classrooms with staff members is an essential step that cannot be skipped. As tempting as it is to "get it done," or say things like, "People are busy, they just want to be told what they should do," taking the time to know and understand the thoughts and ideas of those who will be using the Checkpoints is critical. The true value of our co-creating Checkpoints is not just so each of us can say we've had our fingerprints on our culturized classroom sculpture, the value also comes from USING them as a lens to examine what we are presently seeing from our students and the dispositions and practices we currently employ in our classrooms.

It is conceivable that different schools could land on similar observable Checkpoints after going through the co-creation process. However, we know that each school will be in a different place when it comes to culture. By using our Checkpoints as a specific, formative tool to determine our current state and where we need to go next, we can differentiate for ourselves. We ask teachers to meet the needs of their learners every day—it's time we as school leaders do the same for the hard-working staff members in our schools.

> We ask teachers to meet the needs of their learners every day–it's time we as school leaders do the same for the hard-working staff members in our schools.

Let's head back into a collaborative meeting with Connie and her team, who are thinking about their next steps after creating their Checkpoints for Champion for all Students:

> Thomas: *Our team and the other teams have been working on these Checkpoints for a number of meetings now. One thing I am noticing is that there seems to be a lot that WE need to do. WE need to create opportunities for choice. WE need to assess the different ways that students will show us what they know. WE need to make sure that we are making connections between our content and our students to make it relevant. It sounds like once again, these things have been downloaded onto busy teachers.*
>
> Connie: *Thomas is right, there does seem to be the potential for a lot of heavy lifting for teachers.*
>
> Thomas: *Does this mean that Jennifer is going to just sit back and tell us we need to do more to improve the culture because she is the principal?*
>
> Luis: *I have never gotten the impression that Jennifer isn't willing to roll up her sleeves and get her hands dirty.*
>
> Tamika: *This is where Jennifer said she needed our help. Luis is right, she told us she doesn't just want to be that leader who shouts down from the balcony. She is hoping that we can help her by describing what she might be able to do to help us be successful in implementing our educator Checkpoints. She wants us to add a fourth column to our Checkpoints, one that helps guide her leadership.*
>
> Luis: *I give her credit. She is not shying away from her part in this work.*
>
> Thomas: *Well, let's see how she does once she sees what we need for support. I think it's really important that we have grade level assemblies to*

clarify expectations with all students. Let's put that down, those really set the tone when we did those a few years ago. The kids knew we meant business.

Connie: In truth, I don't know if those assemblies had any long-term effects. When I looked up at students in the crowd, they didn't seem to be paying attention. Not to mention, there were only a few of us sitting with students; the rest of us were standing together around the edge of the gym.

Tamika: I think we need to think more specifically about our educator Checkpoints. The first one we came up with under educators was, "Educators would be using various ways to allow students a choice in how they demonstrate their understanding and thinking." That doesn't really sound like a leader should have an assembly.

Thomas: (chuckling) OK, that's true.

Luis: Giving choice is not as easy as one might think. I try to give choice, but sometimes the students stall out when trying to make a choice. Not to mention, we all have a curriculum to get through.

Thomas: Maybe Jennifer could give us choices at staff meetings. We just sit there for an hour twice a month and listen to boring policies. I know there would be a few things I would change.

Connie: Wait, that's not a bad idea. Thomas, I think you are onto something with that.

Too often we focus on what leadership *looks* like when creating a positive culture in our schools. However, much like the process used earlier with the Core Principles of *Culturize*, school leaders must start with what their actions would LEAD TO for those they lead to help determine what their leadership should look like. This allows administrators (who are also busy people) to prioritize the leadership efforts that truly result in the Checkpoints for culturized classrooms. Let's look at the Champion for Students example created by Connie's collaborative team, specifically the Checkpoints they created for educators:

| Our Educators... |
| --- |
| E1. Using various ways to allow students a choice in how they demonstrate their understanding and thinking. |
| E2. Giving pre-assessments and using ongoing individual conferences and formative assessments to understand what students know, their concerns, interests, and perspectives, so I can connect the learning to them. |
| E3. Working with students to co-create an understanding of the importance of tasks and contexts and model different ways to solve problems. |

Rather than having Jennifer try to assume or guess what leadership that empowers educators to be Champions for Students would look like, Connie and her team have provided Jennifer with specific, descriptive leadership indicators that would help any school leader narrow their focus on how to support and lead their staff. Clarity is not only good for students; it's good for all of us.

Connie's team is modeling what each of the teams in the school can do to create a clear roadmap for administrators to support them in culturizing their classrooms. Rather than listing actions that have vague connections to culture such as "implement grade-level assemblies," "have a logo contest," or "provide resources," the team is using their co-created Checkpoints to form a visible through-line from student-to-educator-to-leader. This helps Jennifer envision the leadership actions needed to make the Checkpoints come to life in their classrooms and throughout the school.

Constructing the leadership actions necessary to support culturizing the classroom is where Robinson's research at the start of this chapter is useful for leaders. While leaders *could* spend their time setting goals for culturizing the classroom, providing resources, planning and coordinating teacher learning, and ensuring a supportive environment, they *should* spend their time promoting and participating in the learning. In other words, if Jennifer wants her teachers to "use various ways to allow students a choice in how they demonstrate their understanding and thinking" (E1) and participate in the learning to do so, she needs to experience what her staff would experience when trying this in their busy classrooms.

For example, Jennifer might research different techniques to give her staff choices in how to demonstrate their learning, model those techniques at staff meetings and professional development days, and then ask her teachers to choose one of the methods she modeled and implement it in their classrooms. Then, by asking teachers to take a picture or video of their students using that choice technique in action and collecting patterns they observed to share with other colleagues, Jennifer and the staff can see the through line that connects their actions to impact when culturizing their classrooms.

Modeling practices during a staff meeting or at a professional development day that teachers can use in their classrooms to help them be Champions for Students or Carry the Banner is the leader's signal to their staff that they are with them. It helps leaders build empathy for what teachers experience in their classrooms in a way that is directly connected to their vision for the culturized classroom. A leader could say, "The staff meeting agenda is pretty busy this week; I don't think I'm going to have time to be able to model giving the staff choice—I'll do it next meeting." But the leader does this at their own peril—it's unreasonable to expect busy teachers to find time in their jam-packed lesson plans to Expect Excellence or be a Merchant of Hope, if the leader isn't willing to do the same in their staff meeting or professional development day plans. Once again, leadership is not a spectator sport. And we ensure it's not a spectator sport by having a set of Checkpoints to guide leaders in the same way we guide our students and educators.

Let's look at what a sample set of leadership Checkpoints could look like:

| Our Educators... | Our Leaders... |
|---|---|
| E1. Using various ways to allow students a choice in how they demonstrate their understanding and thinking. | L1. Researching and modeling ways to provide choice during staff learning events (staff meetings/PD days) and creating protocols/structures for teachers to try and share them with their colleagues. |
| E2. Giving pre-assessments and using ongoing individual conferences and formative assessments to understand what students know, their concerns, interests, and perspectives, so I can connect the learning to them. | L2. Modeling the use of ongoing individual conferences and formative assessment techniques to understand teachers' concerns, interests, and perspectives so the leader can connect the learning to their staff. |
| E3. Working with students to co-create an understanding of the importance of tasks and contexts and model different ways to solve problems. | L3. Working with staff to analyze classroom tasks to ensure they are connected to students and help students to solve problems that are important to them and connected to their context. |

While these Checkpoints would not be the only things that Jennifer and other leaders could do, these specific leader actions are directly connected to the co-created vision of the culturized classroom, much more so than actions such as implement grade-level assemblies, have a logo contest, or provide resources.

In the Matrix below, you will find a process that you can adapt to your own context to help guide you and those in your context to help you move from words on the wall to a set of four-dimensional (student, educator, task/assessment, leader) culturize Checkpoints that might resemble something like this:

| At our school, you will see each of us being 'Champions for Students' when… | | | |
|---|---|---|---|
| Our Students… | Our Educators… | Classroom Tasks/ Assessments ••• | Our Leaders… |
| S1. Are sharing their thinking and understanding in different ways, through discussions, writing, presentations, or using technology. | E1. Are using various ways to allow students choices in how they demonstrate their understanding and thinking. | T1. Allow students to show their learning in more than one way; choice boards; digital student portfolios; presentation-based assessments. | L1. Are researching and modeling ways to provide choice during staff learning events (staff meetings/ PD days) and creating protocols/ structures for teachers to try and share them with their colleagues. |

| At our school, you will see each of us being 'Champions for Students' when... | | | |
|---|---|---|---|
| Our Students... | Our Educators... | Classroom Tasks/ Assessments ••• | Our Leaders... |
| S2. Are telling us what they are doing, why it's important, and how it connects to their lives and experiences. | E2. Are giving pre-assessments and using ongoing individual conferences and formative assessments to understand what students know, their concerns, interests, and perspectives, to connect the learning to them. | T2. Have varied entry points and high exit points; tasks designed with evidence of a connection to student context; assessments that require students to make a claim and support it with evidence, and a personal connection. | L2. Are modeling the use of ongoing individual conferences and formative assessment techniques to understand teachers' concerns, interests, and perspectives so the leader can connect the learning to their staff. |

| At our school, you will see each of us being 'Champions for Students' when... | | | |
|---|---|---|---|
| Our Students... | Our Educators... | Classroom Tasks/ Assessments ... | Our Leaders... |
| S3. Are explaining why it's important for them to complete their work, try it multiple times even if it's hard, and use different strategies to help themselves and others be successful. | E3. Are working with students to co-create an understanding of the importance of tasks and contexts and model different ways to solve problems. | T3. Are multi-step tasks connected to issues that matter to students and their community; assessments that require students to apply multiple problem-solving methods to address an issue that is relevant to their context. | L3. Are working with staff to analyze classroom tasks to ensure they are connected to students and help students to solve problems that are important to them and connected to their context. |

Our vision for what being a Champion for Students leads to for students and what it looks like in our classrooms is now observable. And while we might continue to refine our vision to ensure it passes the Teenager, Civilian, and New Teacher tests for us in our context, we have a co-created starting point that reflects our thoughts, knowledge, and beliefs about this and the other Core Principles of the culturized classroom in our context.

A question we often hear at this point is, "This sounds OK, but how much time is this going to take?" This is a reasonable question, and the answer is: "It depends." It is our contention that if we truly believe that culture is a collective responsibility, we need to do our best to ensure that the collective is involved at all phases of the design and implementation of Culturize Checkpoints. In other words, we need to provide adequate time and space to understand where we are at, where we need to go next, and to work and learn together in a consistent way that builds culture while defining culture in our context.

In addition, we would be naive not to mention that we recognize that each school has a different set of realities. Some individuals or teams may find themselves feeling isolated, alone, and wondering how they might be able to have an impact on culturizing their classrooms when others may not have the same desire or commitment. However, we also believe there are things that remain within your sphere of influence, including finding someone in your school who would want to partner with you to identify Checkpoints and then ask that individual or others to observe you and provide feedback. We also often encourage staff to share their frustrations/experiences with administration and seek their advice on next steps. This can lead to a partnership with your administration or opportunities for professional leave to attend a training or visit another colleague at another school. Whether you are the only person in your school who teaches your content or you are surrounded by a team of colleagues, our suggestion is to start small (perhaps with just one of the Core Principles) and use a combination of individual reflection points, joint prep times, grade-level, content, or other collaborative team meetings, staff meetings, professional learning opportunities, and finally, request release time to work with other members of your staff. A sample roadmap with a sequencing of meetings might look something like this:

- **Staff Meeting #1:** Introduction to the four Core Principles of *Culturize*/Determining Our *Culturize* Focus:

- Brief summary and knowledge building around the four Core Principles
- Provocation Question for Collaborative Teams discussion: "If we were to focus on ONE of the four Core Principles from *Culturize*, which one do we believe would have the biggest impact on our current culture in our school?"

- **Collaborative Team Meeting #1:** Teams discuss the Core Principles, and then individual prioritization followed by team consensus building on which Core Principle represents the best start point for the school.
- **Staff Meeting #2:** Staff consensus building: selection of the Core Principle ranked as the highest priority for the school as described by each team, followed by action planning and next steps.
- **Professional Development Opportunity #1:** Whole staff together develops the first draft of the four-dimensional (student, educator, task, leader) vision of the Priority Core Principle.
- **Collaboration Team Meeting #2:** Teams re-visit the draft vision of the Priority Core Principle through the lens of the Teenager Test, Civilian Test, and New Teacher test and make edits/additions as needed.
- **Staff Meeting #3:** Staff finalizes the Priority Core Principle vision, and begins the process of narrowing the focus for each collaborative team.
  - Provocation Question for Collaborative Teams discussion: "If there were *one* aspect from the educator (E) or task (T) of our Priority Core Principle that we would like to learn more about as a team, which one would it be?"
- **Collaboration Team Meeting #3:** Each team selects one aspect from the educator (E) or task (T) portion of the Priority Core Principle and maps out a culturize learning cycle for the next

6-8 weeks to learn, design, implement, observe, and document a new team approach to culturizing their classroom.

+ **Staff Meeting #4:** A quick, mid-cycle "Heat Check" to check-in on each team to see how they are progressing and what supports they might need.

+ **Staff Meeting #5:** A team *Culturize My Classroom Impact Sharing Celebration* where teams share the impact of the strategy they chose to culturize their classroom with other teams in the school.

+ **Instructional Leadership Team Reflection Meeting:** School leadership and team leaders meet to reflect on how the culturize learning cycle went, the impact the cycle had on the culture of classrooms and the school as a whole, and what improvements could be made to the cycle to increase the observable impact of the work that had been done by teams to culturize their classrooms.

Again, this is just a *possible* sequence of meetings. Each of the items above are not meant to take up an entire staff meeting or an entire professional development day. We know how valuable and time-crunched some of these structures can be. However, by keeping our work on culture as a consistent component of meetings and learning opportunities, we make it part of our culture to collectively work on culture.

Without question, this process takes time and effort, so mapping out a timeline of events is crucial for clarity, consistency, and staying the course. When we do not have a clear focus of who we want to be and have not come to agreement on how we are going to behave, we run

HAVING a vision is not the same as USING the vision to tell us where we are at and where we need to go next.

the risk of moving from words on the wall to MORE words on the wall. In as much as we garner a greater depth of knowledge of the Core Principles of the culturized classroom, HAVING a vision is not the same as USING the vision to tell us where we are at and where we need to go next.

## PRESS PAUSE MOMENT: REFLECTION SPACE

+

+

+

## CHAPTER 4

~

# Please. Not. One.
# More. Initiative.

*"If you spend your life trying to be good at everything,*
*you will never be great at anything."*

—Tom Rath

Take a moment to reflect upon all the initiatives that you
have been expected to implement in your career. In reading,
writing, and numeracy. Around Social Emotional Learning,
virtual learning, and behavior intervention systems. Learning manage-
ment systems, grading programs, and parent communication software.
High-tech stuff, low-tech stuff, and everything in between. While we
may talk of all the shortages we might see in education, the one thing
that educators new and experienced can agree upon is that there is no
shortage of initiatives in our school systems.

In 1998, tech writer Linda Stone coined the term "continuous
partial attention" a term to describe a modern adaptive behavior of
continuously dividing one's attention over multiple tasks. In her blog,
Stone says, "We pay continuous partial attention in an effort NOT TO
MISS ANYTHING. It is an always-on, anywhere, anytime, anyplace

behavior that involves an artificial sense of constant crisis. We are always on high alert when we pay continuous partial attention." She goes on to say that continuous partial attention can lead to over-stimulation, lack of fulfillment, and an increased sense of powerlessness.[8] Sounds a lot like our schools at certain points, doesn't it?

In reading the first few chapters of this book, you would not be wrong in asking, "How are we supposed to do all this stuff?" As important as we might think it is to culturize the classroom, trying to take on the four Core Principles of *Culturize* all at once, in the lives of busy educators, epitomizes the need for continuous partial attention. Not to mention, some of the most important elements of the Core Principles are already happening in our classrooms today. Considering the ever-increasing catalog of things educators and leaders are tasked to do in our schools, we need to ensure that we do what is expected for our students, but neglected for our adults: we need to meet **educators** where they are at.

Frequently when we are beginning our work on something as important and all-encompassing as culturizing the classroom, we can be tempted to start with a question like, "Where are we at?" or, "What's the current state of affairs with

> Considering the ever-increasing catalog of things educators and leaders are tasked to do in our schools, we need to ensure that we do what is expected for our students, but neglected for our adults: we need to meet educators where they are at.

[8] *Businessweek - Bloomberg.* Bloomberg.com. (2008, July 24). http://www.businessweek.com/business_at_work/time_management/archives/2008/07/continuous_part.html

culture in our school?" Starting with where we are at is important; however, if we don't have common language for what we mean by things such as being a Champion for Students or Carrying the Banner, the answers to these questions can cause confusion and rarely tell us where we need to go next. This is where the process of co-creating Culturize Checkpoints is key; we have developed a common language that allows us to more accurately assess the status of culture in our school and narrow our focus for the first steps that make the most sense for us in our context.

Let's look back at the student Checkpoints created by Connie and her team:

| Our Students... |
|---|
| S1. Are sharing their thinking and understanding in different ways, through discussions, writing, presentations, or using technology. |
| S2. Are telling us what they are doing, why it's important, and how it connects to their lives and experiences. |
| S3. Are explaining why it's important for them to complete their work, try it multiple times even if it's hard, and different strategies to help themselves and others be successful. |

Considering your students, how often would you estimate they demonstrate these Checkpoints in your classroom? For convenience, we can use a frequency scale called the CSN scale: (C)onsistently (S) ometimes (N)ot Yet. If you look at the descriptors above, what would you estimate to be the frequency of this occurring in your context? You might choose to be even more specific, using phrases such as "7 of my 19 students can consistently tell me what they are doing, why they are doing it, and how it connects to their lives and experiences." As a result of our Checkpoints, we now have a much higher level of specificity when describing the current state of Championing for Students through the lens of our students. The more clarity we have around where we are at, the more clarity we have with our first steps.

Perhaps your responses looked something like this:

| Our Students... |
| --- |
| S1. Are sharing their thinking and understanding in different ways, through discussions, writing, presentations, or using technology. **SOMETIMES** |
| S2. Are telling us what they are doing, why it's important, and how it connects to their lives and experiences. **SOMETIMES** |
| S3. Are explaining why it's important for them to complete their work, try it multiple times even if it's hard, and different strategies to help themselves and others be successful. **NOT YET** |

Knowing where our students are at is one part of the picture when it comes to framing our current culture status. Examining the rest of the picture is where it can begin to become less comfortable for us as adults because it requires us to move from the microscope to the mirror. Not only do we need to name and acknowledge what we are seeing from our students, we also must examine our current actions as educators, the tasks and assessments we presently use in our classrooms, and the existing leadership supports that are leading to the culture that we have in our building.

Looking at our own practice often leads to different reactions and feelings. We can feel defensive and overwhelmed. We can point fingers and blame. We can feel embarrassed and self-conscious. We can throw our hands in the air, say things like, "We're already working as hard as we can!" and be tempted to give up. Please know that if you are beginning to feel any or all of these, it is not only natural, it shows that you believe in what you are doing and want what is best for students in your classroom.

However, if together we can truly embrace the idea that (through our actions, tasks, and leadership) we cause culture, we become empowered. By knowing what we can do and where we are at with each of the Checkpoints on our culturize trajectory, we can begin to chart a course that makes sense for our school.

Let's check in with Connie and the rest of her team. Connie and the other team leaders have recently met with Principal Jennifer, who has introduced them to the idea of assessing the current state of the Core Principles in their classrooms using their Culturize Checkpoints and the CSN scale:

*Tamika: It's been a lot of work, but I am excited at the progress that we've made in creating Checkpoints for Champion for Students. I thought the work that other teams shared at the last staff meeting was quite good as well. For the first time, I feel like, as a staff, we have a better understanding of what the Core Principles can look like for us.*

*Thomas: It should be pretty good at this point, we've spent enough time on it. But now that we've done this work, what are we supposed to do with it? Are we just putting up bigger posters in our classrooms? I don't think the kids have noticed the last ones.*

*Connie: Jennifer asked our team to use our Checkpoints to see how often they are occurring in our classrooms using that CSN frequency scale: Consistently, Sometimes or Not Yet. She wanted us to use different letters on our Checkpoint Matrix; C for consistently," S for "sometimes," and N for "not yet."*

*Thomas: This will be easy for me. I will mark N for the kids and C for us and our tasks. We keep leading the horses to water, but we can't make 'em drink it. Is there a different letter for leaders that we can use for "We have no idea what they do"?*

*Luis: My kids are not all N's, and as a teacher, I'm trying but not consistent with all these. I have a lot to learn.*

*Connie: That's what Jennifer said this is all about—not blaming students or feeling bad as adults; it's about us being honest about where we are at so we can find out where we want to go next as teams.*

*Tamika: Besides, if each one of the educators were doing each of these things all the time, I don't think we would be talking about the issues people say we currently have with our culture.*

*Luis: We should do this independently first, and then see if we are on the same page.*

Using your own set of Culturize Checkpoints to conduct a formative assessment of the current state of Champion for Students, pretend that you are one of the members of Connie's team in this meeting.

Considering your own classroom or context and the C-S-N responses you created for students above, use the matrix in the reflection space below to consider how frequently you can implement the educator and task/assessment Checkpoints in your classroom or context. Write (C)onsistently, (S)ometimes or (N)ot yet at the bottom of each of the boxes. Use the same C-S-N scale to describe your perceptions of how often your administrator demonstrates the Leader Checkpoints in your school. (If you are a school leader, do the same for your classrooms, but take a more global, school-wide perspective.)

## PRESS PAUSE MOMENT: REFLECTION SPACE

♦

♦

♦

| At our school, you will see each of us being 'Champions for Students' when… | | | |
|---|---|---|---|
| Our students… | Our Educators… | Classroom Tasks/ Assessments ♦♦♦ | Our Leaders… |
| S1. Are sharing their thinking and understanding in different ways, through discussions, writing, presentations, or using technology. | E1. Are using various ways to allow students choices in how they demonstrate their understanding and thinking. | T1. Allow students to show their learning in more than one way; choice boards; digital student portfolios; presentation-based assessments. | L1. Are researching and modeling ways to provide choice during staff learning events (staff meetings/ PD days) and creating protocols/ structures for teachers to try and share them with their colleagues. |

| At our school, you will see each of us being 'Champions for Students' when… | | | |
|---|---|---|---|
| Our students… | Our Educators… | Classroom Tasks/ Assessments ••• | Our Leaders… |
| S2. Are telling us what they are doing, why it's important, and how it connects to their lives and experiences. | E2. Are giving pre-assessments and using ongoing individual conferences and formative assessments to understand what students know, their concerns, interests, and perspectives, to connect the learning to them. | T2. Have varied entry points and high exit points; tasks designed with evidence of a connection to student context; assessments that require students to make a claim and support it with evidence, and a personal connection. | L2. Are modeling the use of ongoing individual conferences and formative assessment techniques to understand teachers' concerns, interests, and perspectives so the leader can connect the learning to their staff. |

| At our school, you will see each of us being 'Champions for Students' when... | | | |
|---|---|---|---|
| Our students... | Our Educators... | Classroom Tasks/ Assessments ... | Our Leaders... |
| S3. Are explaining why it's important for them to complete their work, try it multiple times even if it's hard, and different strategies to help themselves and others be successful. | E3. Are working with students to co-create an understanding of the importance of tasks and contexts and model different ways to solve problems. | T3. Are multistep tasks connected to issues that matter to students and their community; assessments that require students to apply multiple problem-solving methods to address an issue that is relevant to their context. | L3. Are working with staff to analyze classroom tasks to ensure they are connected to students and help students to solve problems that are important to them and connected to their context. |

Maybe your matrix looked something like this:

| At our school, you will see each of us being 'Champions for Students' when... | | | |
|---|---|---|---|
| **Our Students...** | **Our Educators...** | **Classroom Tasks/ Assessments ...** | **Our Leaders...** |
| S1. Are sharing their thinking and under-standing in different ways, through discus-sions, writing, presentations, or using technology. | E1. Are using various ways to allow students choices in how they demon-strate their understanding and thinking. | T1. Allow students to show their learning in more than one way; choice boards; digital student port-folios; presen-tation-based assessments. | L1. Are researching and modeling ways to provide choice during staff learning events (staff meetings/PD days) and creat-ing protocols/ structures for teachers to try and share them with their colleagues. |
| **Consistently** | **Consistently** | **Consistently** | Not Yet |

| At our school, you will see each of us being 'Champions for Students' when… | | | |
|---|---|---|---|
| Our Students… | Our Educators… | Classroom Tasks/ Assessments … | Our Leaders… |
| S2. Are telling us what they are doing, why it's important, and how it connects to their lives and experiences. | E2. Are giving pre-assessments and using ongoing individual conferences and formative assessments to understand what students know, their concerns, interests, and perspectives, so they can connect the learning to them. | T2. Have varied entry points and high exit points; tasks designed with evidence of a connection to student context; assessments that require students to make a claim and support it with evidence, and a personal connection. | L2. Are modeling the use of ongoing individual conferences and formative assessment techniques to understand teachers' concerns, interests, and perspectives so the leader can connect the learning to their staff. |
| Not Yet | Sometimes | Not Yet | Sometimes |

| At our school, you will see each of us being 'Champions for Students' when… | | | |
|---|---|---|---|
| Our Students… | Our Educators… | Classroom Tasks/ Assessments … | Our Leaders… |
| S3. Are explaining why it's important for them to complete their work, try it multiple times even if it's hard, and different strategies to help themselves and others be successful. | E3. Are working with students to co-create an understanding of the importance of tasks and contexts and model different ways to solve problems. | T3. Are multi-step tasks connected to issues that matter to students and their community; assessments that require students to apply multiple problem-solving methods to address an issue that is relevant to their context. | L3. Are working with staff to analyze classroom tasks to ensure they are connected to students and help students to solve problems that are important to them and connected to their context. |
| Sometimes | Consistently | Sometimes | Not Yet |

Let's jump back in with Connie's team, who has just put their Checkpoints up on the wall in their Team Room:

*Connie: OK, wow. So what are we noticing?*

*Thomas: Not a lot of C's from the kids. And truthfully, not a lot of C's from the adults or the tasks either. I'm a bit surprised. We're hard on ourselves.*

*Tamika: It's just like when we ask our kids to assess themselves—I usually find them to be harder on themselves than I am.*

*Luis: I am pretty surprised at how similar ours came out. I think we feel like we are fairly consistent in being Champions for Students by allowing them to demonstrate their learning in different ways.*

*Connie: We're also pretty consistent in thinking that our students don't always know why they are doing some of the things that we have them do in our classrooms. Tamika, you had a different thought. You rated students as consistently on "telling us what they are doing, why they are doing it, and how it connects to their lives." What are you seeing that makes you say that?*

*Tamika: Actually, Jennifer did a Checkpoint walkthrough of my class a few weeks ago, and she said that each student was able to tell her what they were learning about. (Tamika pauses) But now that I think about it, that describes my kids; they can tell me what they are doing, but I don't think they can connect it to their own context yet. I might need to change that to "sometimes" instead.*

*Luis: When we look at each of ours up on the wall, it looks to me like our kids can show us what they know, but they can't really tell us why it's important.*

*Connie: Totally agree. I do labs with them—they love mixing things and burning things with the Bunsen burners. But after the lab when I ask them about what they've learned, they don't talk about the importance of the Law of Conservation of Mass, they would rather talk about how much the class smelled like burnt peanuts.*

*Thomas: The Law of Conservation of Mass isn't important to most teenagers. If it's not about social media, it doesn't matter.*

*Luis: I think there are lots of things that are important to kids. But how much time do we actually spend getting to know what's important to each of our students?*

*Thomas: Well, that's true, my own kids' interests change from week to week. But the one other thing we all seem to agree on is that our leadership team really needs to start walking the walk.*

Having discussions during which teams are using Checkpoints and language they have created to analyze, compare, contrast, make predictions, and consider their practice around culturizing their classrooms represents an important marker when moving from words on the wall to having an observable impact on the culture of the school.

Imagine the level of clarity around the current state of a school's culture if each teacher was to do their own classroom Checkpoint "heat map." To determine: If each teacher team was having dialogue using specific, descriptive co-created language about culture. If teams from across the school came together to share what they were seeing from their students, themselves, their tasks, and the leadership support. Imagine if, after the hard work of Connie's team and all the other teams and the guidance of Principal Jennifer, the staff were to create a consolidated Checkpoint Heat Map that looked something like this:

| At our school, you will see each of us being CHAMPIONS FOR STUDENTS when... | | | |
|---|---|---|---|
| Our Students... | Our Educators... | Classroom Tasks/Assessments... | Our Leaders... |
| S | C | N | N |
| N | S | N | S |
| S | C | S | N |

| At our school, you will see each of us EXPECTING EXCELLENCE when... | | | |
|---|---|---|---|
| Our Students... | Our Educators... | Classroom Tasks/Assessments... | Our Leaders... |
| C | C | S | S |
| N | N | N | N |
| C | C | S | C |

| At our school, you will see each of us CARRYING THE BANNER when... | | | |
|---|---|---|---|
| Our Students... | Our Educators... | Classroom Tasks/Assessments... | Our Leaders... |
| C | C | S | C |
| S | S | S | S |
| N | S | S | N |

| At our school, you will see each of us being MERCHANTS OF HOPE when... | | | |
|---|---|---|---|
| Our Students... | Our Educators... | Classroom Tasks/Assessments... | Our Leaders... |
| N | S | N | S |
| N | S | N | S |
| N | N | N | N |

Even without seeing the school's specific Culturize Checkpoints, what could the teachers and leaders learn from a Checkpoint heat map that looked like this? Knowing that **C** represents Consistently and **N** represents Not Yet, what are some of the patterns that Jennifer and her teams could determine? In the reflection space below, jot down potential themes the school could identify from this heat map, considering:

+ Core principle areas of strength and stretches
+ Student trends, strengths, and stretches
+ Educator trends, strengths, and stretches
+ Task/assessment trends, strengths, and stretches
+ Leadership trends, strengths, and stretches
+ Hint: look holistically and vertically.

## PRESS PAUSE MOMENT: REFLECTION SPACE

+

+

+

You might have come up with patterns such as, "Teachers and leaders have determined:

- that students demonstrate Checkpoints more frequently in Expecting Excellence and Carrying the Banner and less frequently in Merchants of Hope and Champions for Students
- that teachers and leaders most frequently demonstrate Checkpoints in Carrying the Banner and less frequently demonstrate Checkpoints in Merchants of Hope
- that across the four Core Principles, the strand where Checkpoints are being demonstrated least frequently is "Classroom Tasks and Assessments"
- Carrying the Banner #1 and #3 are the Checkpoints most frequently observed in students, educators, tasks, and leadership
- Expecting Excellence #2 and Merchant of Hope #3 are the Checkpoints least frequently observed in students, educators, tasks, and leadership

By clarifying our status with Checkpoints, we can specifically acknowledge our school's strengths and stretches. This is not to make us feel poorly about what we are currently doing. It's to acknowledge the fact that teachers and leaders are busy, and everyone is in a different starting place. Imagine if we put the Checkpoint Heat Map beside one created by a nearby school in the district:

# Jennifer and Connie's school:

| At our school, you will see each of us being CHAMPIONS FOR STUDENTS when... | | | |
|---|---|---|---|
| Our Students... | Our Educators... | Classroom Tasks/Assessments... | Our Leaders... |
| S | C | N | N |
| N | S | N | S |
| S | C | S | N |

| At our school, you will see each of us EXPECTING EXCELLENCE when... | | | |
|---|---|---|---|
| Our Students... | Our Educators... | Classroom Tasks/Assessments... | Our Leaders... |
| C | C | S | S |
| N | N | N | N |
| C | C | S | C |

| At our school, you will see each of us CARRYING THE BANNER when... | | | |
|---|---|---|---|
| Our Students... | Our Educators... | Classroom Tasks/Assessments... | Our Leaders... |
| C | C | S | C |
| S | S | S | S |
| N | S | S | N |

| At our school, you will see each of us being MERCHANTS OF HOPE when... | | | |
|---|---|---|---|
| Our Students... | Our Educators... | Classroom Tasks/Assessments... | Our Leaders... |
| N | S | N | S |
| N | S | N | S |
| N | N | N | N |

# Neighboring School:

| At our school, you will see each of us being CHAMPIONS FOR STUDENTS when... | | | |
|---|---|---|---|
| Our Students... | Our Educators... | Classroom Tasks/Assessments... | Our Leaders... |
| N | S | N | S |
| N | S | N | S |
| N | S | N | N |

| At our school, you will see each of us EXPECTING EXCELLENCE when... | | | |
|---|---|---|---|
| Our Students... | Our Educators... | Classroom Tasks/Assessments... | Our Leaders... |
| C | C | S | N |
| S | S | S | S |
| C | C | S | C |

| At our school, you will see each of us CARRYING THE BANNER when... | | | |
|---|---|---|---|
| Our Students... | Our Educators... | Classroom Tasks/Assessments... | Our Leaders... |
| S | S | N | N |
| N | S | N | S |
| N | N | N | N |

| At our school, you will see each of us being MERCHANTS OF HOPE when... | | | |
|---|---|---|---|
| Our Students... | Our Educators... | Classroom Tasks/Assessments... | Our Leaders... |
| S | C | S | S |
| C | C | C | S |
| C | C | S | C |

A potential starting point for learning at each of these schools would likely be quite different. Jennifer's school might choose to target their next work around their Merchant of Hope Checkpoints, whereas the neighboring school could see Champion for Students as a more natural starting point to best meet the needs of their students, teachers, and leaders.

While there can be varying starting points between schools, there can also be varying starting points WITHIN schools. Teams are in different places, and teachers are, too. The two heat maps above could also represent different teacher teams, but the message is the same. Earlier in the chapter, we talked about the role of the leader in moving culture from words on the wall to action and impact. To this point, through Jennifer, Connie, and her collaborative team, we have outlined a process for schools to determine what culturizing the classroom leads to in students and what the teaching, tasks, and leadership could look like as a result—our desired state. We have described a heat-mapping process to help schools determine their current state in a way that is specific and descriptive in surfacing school-specific next steps. We are on our way.

At this point, once again, it might be tempting for us to just dive in and tackle each of the Core Principles all at once. As educators, we are problem-solvers, and because we know that the next big initiative is likely hurtling down the pike toward us, we can sometimes try to get it all done right now. However, rekindling the culture of our schools is not a box that can be checked. As leaders and educators, we know that too often we go wide in certain areas when we actually need to go deep. Looking at something as complex as culture is one of those areas that requires us to dig deeper, not wider.

We have spent some time describing "what" culturizing our classrooms would lead to and look like. In the next chapters, we are going to dig into the "how"—the *practice* of culturizing the classroom through the lenses of each of the four Core Principles.

# CHAPTER 5

# Enough with the WHY and the WHAT...Tell me HOW.

*"The deepest irony of American education is that the institutions that are responsible for learning in our society do the worst job of enabling the learning of the people who work in them."*

—Richard Elmore, *Instructional Rounds in Education*

Time for professional learning for teachers is precious. No matter how many PD days, collaborative meetings, or snippets of staff meetings that we can carve out of the school year for teachers to hone and reflect upon teaching and learning, there never is (and likely never will be) enough time. How many of us have engaged in these informal types of professional learning?

+ Copy Room PD: The quick chats with a colleague while waiting for the copy machine, or (bonus) when someone has left something on the photocopier that looks like something we could use in our classroom.

- Filing Cabinet PD: Thumbing through the files of teachers present and past for tried and tested ideas for teaching concepts and standards.
- Hallway Supervision PD: A louder, often interrupted version of Copy Room PD where brief exchanges of ideas are usually accompanied by a between-class snack or cup of coffee.
- One-Hit-Wonder PD: Something that disappears as quickly as it shows up (also known as SnapChat PD for those unfamiliar with the term One-Hit-Wonder).

Then there are the full-day professional learning sessions we have on the calendar. While these longer sessions can be impactful, we must be cautious in how we design them. Because they happen less frequently, we tend to pack them full. Too often, teachers and leaders walk away from PD days with their heads spinning, unclear, and overwhelmed with the task of trying to figure out how this next great thing fits onto their already full plates. It's no wonder we often find ourselves commiserating with our colleagues shortly after.

In *Navigating Leadership Drift* (2023), McDowell and Birk ask leaders to consider an approach to designing engaging professional learning for educators called "need it – see it – start it – show it" (NSSS). They contend that when educators:

- *Need* the change
- Can *see* what the change will look like in their context
- Can *start* the change because it meets them where they are at
- Must *show* the change and how it met their needs

they are much more likely to implement strategies and approaches gleaned from professional learning in their classrooms.[9]

---

[9] McDowell, M. & Birk, C. (2023). *Navigating Leadership Drift: Observable Impact On Rigorous Learning*. FIRST Educational Resources, LLC.

If you have already read *Culturize* and are still reading this book, you have likely seen the need to re-establish a positive culture in your context. You and your colleagues may have observed that your students are not demonstrating certain behaviors or expected learning outcomes. You might have noticed that some adults no longer want to be a part of committees or are less willing to participate in activities that helped shape the culture of the school in previous years. The leadership in the school might have changed, and maybe it seems like a good time to recalibrate collective commitments to school culture. Or perhaps there is another reason; regardless, you have felt a need to examine and rekindle your culture that currently feels dormant.

In the previous chapters, we've outlined the process of co-creating Culturize Checkpoints in an attempt to help us think about what the Core Principles lead to and look like for us in our context, and to make our beliefs, thoughts, and ideas about culture observable so we can see where we need to go next. But culturizing the classroom and having our observables on paper is one thing, seeing it in action is quite another. The more clarity we can bring to the "see it" portion of need it - see it - start it - show it, the more likely we are to loop people into getting started on culturizing the classroom.

Let's rejoin Connie and her collaborative team at their weekly meeting, where Thomas is struggling to get started with the work of culturizing the classroom:

*Thomas: I won't lie, I'm still skeptical about this whole Checkpoint thing. All this stuff sounds good on paper, but once again, teachers are left to figure out how to do it in their classrooms. I get the idea that we want to change our culture. I get the idea that it's not just up to kids. What I don't get is how to take all this stuff and make it happen while I'm trying to get our kids to pass tests in science.*

*Connie: I hear what you are saying; there is a lot to look at here. But I haven't gotten the impression that Jennifer wants us to do all of this, all at once. I think what she is hoping is that we can use our Checkpoints to look for opportunities to be Champions for Students or to Carry the Banner in our classrooms.*

*Tamika: Luis, I know that you have had some success in your classrooms in implementing some of the Checkpoints. Did you do it all at once, pick one Checkpoint to focus on, or a combination of a few? How did you do it?*

*Luis: I know what Thomas is saying. When I first looked at our school Checkpoints, I thought it might be easy for our staff to become overwhelmed. So I looked at the heat map we created and decided to focus on one aspect that I wanted to see from each of my students. I really wanted them to understand the "why," to see the importance of what we do. And not just in science either. I think kids ask, "Why?" in every class, so if we can help each other in different departments, why wouldn't we?*

*Thomas: If you can figure out the "why" for kids, you should get a Nobel Peace Prize. Invite me to your classroom when that happens. I need to see that in action.*

*Luis: Well, I don't have it figured out, but I am using individual conferencing in my classes to get to know my kids a bit better, to find out what makes them tick, to try and find ways to connect them to learning, and now I'm using them as a check for understanding, too.*

*Tamika: It would be great if we had more opportunities to observe different teachers and how they are making the Checkpoints a part of their classroom. I would like to see what Luis is doing.*

*Luis: It's nothing fancy, but sure. I think my students would enjoy that. I have also heard that Carol is doing some really great things in fifth grade in Math. What if we all went to observe her as a team?*

*Thomas: I don't know if she would appreciate it if all of us were there, why don't you folks go? I can hang back and do it another time.*

*Connie: Are you kidding? Carol just asked a bunch of the Grade 4 team teachers to help her by observing some of this work in her classroom a few weeks ago. I think she will be fine with it. I will check with her.*

Richard Elmore's quote at the start of the chapter should give us pause for thought. It is ironic that the learning for teachers in our schools can be sporadic, fragmented, in sit-and-get format and usually takes place outside of the classroom without students (Would it be ideal to have a golfer practice in a conference room? A chef in a lecture theater?).

This past year, a school leader said, "It's a shame that as the principal, I seem to be the one who gets the most professional learning. My job allows me to be released and gives me the freedom to see different classrooms. I want to change that." He was determined to find different ways to give his staff opportunities to be able to see teaching and learning in action during the school day. He wanted to create opportunities for his teachers to observe classrooms.

Classroom observations can play a central role in making teaching and learning more visible. They can help expose teachers to different approaches they might not have tried before and also help new and experienced teachers become more aware of how their interactions affect their students.[10] However, for classroom observations to have an

---

[10] Halim, S, Wahid, R. and Halim, T. (2018). Classroom Observation- A Powerful Tool for Continuous Professional Development (CPD). International Journal on Language, Research and Education Studies. 2. 162-168. 10.30575/2017/IJLRES-2018050801.

impact by having us assess, reflect upon, and even alter our practices, we must go beyond just providing the time and opportunity for teachers to get out of their classrooms.

Time for teachers is a valuable commodity. Teachers are (rightfully) protective of the time to be with their own students, so we want to make it count when they are observing their colleagues. In addition, because getting out of our classrooms tends to be rare, it can feel like we are trying to see Disneyworld in a single day. We want to ensure that our observations are tightly focused on what it is we want to learn more about.

There are a few key elements we must consider for Checkpoint Walkthroughs to be impactful:

1. *Checkpoint Walkthroughs must be safe.* When we walk through classrooms to look for our Culturize Checkpoints, there should be no connection to evaluation. We have seen the negative long-term impact this can have on a school's culture in terms of trust when administrators later include these Checkpoints in their summative evaluation of a teacher. Checkpoint walkthroughs are meant to be additional sets of eyes to provide the classroom teacher with insights that might be difficult to notice when they are busy teaching in the classroom. As a result, Checkpoint Walkthroughs must be specifically focused on an agreed-upon set of co-created Checkpoints.
   + Suggestions:
     ◇ Walkthroughs are an important piece of culturizing the classroom. Although we believe that all teachers should participate in this process, we recognize teachers may be at different levels of readiness. We can differentiate this experience by having people begin with helping to create Checkpoints, being observers, recording themselves, watching their videos with a colleague, and,

98

finally, moving to a place where they are comfortable being observed in their own classroom. With this differentiated approach, the goal is for each teacher to have the experience of modeling aspects of culturizing for observable impact in their classrooms.

- Have staff post a QR code with their Culturize Checkpoint focus area for their upcoming unit on their door for observers.
- Post "This Week's Culturize Checkpoint look fors" in the weekly staff bulletin to let teachers know about a weekly Checkpoint focus.
- Have those who are hesitant about being observed begin as observers first. It's a great way to start the peer observation process.

2. *Checkpoint Walkthroughs and observations must be objective, without judgment, and specific to the agreed-upon Checkpoints from the Core Principles.* This is where having co-created Checkpoints like Jennifer and her team created together is essential. If a collaborative team or individual teacher has invited us to observe their classroom and they indicate that their areas of focus for a walkthrough are Champions for Students *S1: students are sharing their thinking and understanding in different ways* and *E1: educators are using various ways to give students choice in demonstrating a standard*, observations and feedback should be geared towards these two areas. We should not add other unsolicited feedback.

- Suggestions:
  - Use your co-created Checkpoints—this is what they are for.
  - Have a pre-Checkpoint Walkthrough meeting with observers and those to be observed to calibrate the observers and the types of observations to be provided.

- At a faculty meeting, provide opportunities for teams to practice giving specific, descriptive feedback related to the Checkpoint ("2 of 7 students were able to share their thinking in more than one way" vs. "our students struggled to show me what they knew")
- Think "I am the cameraperson, not the journalist. I'm here to act as another set of eyes, not editorialize on what I believe is best."

3. *Checkpoint Walkthroughs and observations must be beneficial for the observed AND the observer:* If time is precious for teachers, pulling them out of their classrooms must lead to something that is going to help them. If a teacher wants to provide more choices for their students, sending them to do an observation on the way a teacher does individual conferencing is not necessarily the best use of their time. Furthermore, the person who is being observed should also get something from the visit: specific, descriptive feedback about the Culturize Checkpoint they wanted to observe, and potential ideas about what the next steps might be for continued growth.
   - Suggestions:
     - Have a "Culturize Checkpoint Matchmaker," a list of host teachers who are working on a particular Checkpoint or Core Principle and are willing to be hosts to other teachers, next to a list of guest teachers who want to learn more about developing a particular Checkpoint and be 'guests' in a host classroom
     - Have quarterly or semesterly, small group "Culturize Celebrations" where educators can share ideas and strategies at staff meetings or professional learning days.

4. *Checkpoint Walkthroughs must be ongoing:* Checkpoint Walk-throughs are not meant to be an event nor a dog and pony show. The goal is not to do our best lesson, but rather to have other sets of eyes to help us connect our actions to the impact they have on our students. If we truly want to culturize our classrooms, it should become part of our culture that we want to learn from each other.

   + Suggestions:
     ◇ Have shorter, but more frequent, observations. Much can be learned in fifteen minutes when we have specific Checkpoints to look for, and the more observations we do, the better we get at it.
     ◇ Include paraprofessionals in the observation process—the insights we can gain from our paraprofessionals are remarkable and underutilized.

Finally, Checkpoint Walkthroughs should be (gasp) enjoyable. Seeing our peers in action, visiting with other students and learning more about how we can create a positive culture in our schools are the things that make education enjoyable. If we approach Checkpoint Walkthroughs with a curious "I wonder what I can learn?" mentality where we can be that other set of eyes for our peers and learn more about something we value, it's a great way to spend part of the day.

Let's rejoin Connie's collaborative team having a short meeting with Carol before observing in her classroom later in the day:

*Connie: Carol, I'm so excited you are willing to have our team come to your classroom after lunch.*

*Thomas: Are you sure you are OK with all of us coming? I can see how a bunch of observers might make a teacher or the students feel uncomfortable.*

*Carol: No no, it's great. Truthfully, our staff Checkpoints have made me think differently about my lessons. I need some help to know if what I am doing is making a difference. To have your team there will be helpful for me. The other team that came through gave me lots of useful feedback. And my students stated they enjoyed sharing their learnings with everyone.*

*Tamika: Carol, what would you like us to look for in your classroom? What has been your area of focus?*

*Carol: I have been working on incorporating parts of Champion for Students in my lessons. Specifically, I know you might find this hard to believe, but I have struggled with getting Grade 5 students to connect to the "why" of math. (the group laughs) That's where S2 from our Checkpoints really hit home with me.*

*Luis (looking at his Checkpoint sheet): That's "telling us what they are doing, why it's important and how it connects to their lives and experiences," right?*

*Carol: Exactly, so when you come to my classroom, I need you to see if they are able to show you what they are learning, and then be able to describe how it connects to something that is important to them. I've been conferencing with them individually at least once per two-week cycle so I can check in with them but also get to know what interests them. Then I am trying to take activities and give them as much choice as I can using ideas they told me they connect to.*

*Thomas: That conferencing sounds like a lot of work.*

*Carol: Actually, it's not too bad—I got some ideas from Jennifer. I noticed that she chats with one or two of us every staff meeting, so I decided to try the same strategy with my students. And you know what? The kids like it—one of my students would barely make eye contact with me at the start of the year. Now she babbles on and on to me about golf.*

*Luis: So just to be clear, you want us to observe two things for you, correct? First, the different ways and how often students show their learning. And second, if they can tell us what they are learning and why it's important?*

*Carol: Specific feedback around those points would be perfect. But one more thing. I would love to know what you observe the students doing as a result of what I am doing—what do you notice from the kids when they have choices? Giving choice is not always easy, but if it pays off, I am all in. Here's an outline of the lesson, just so you can have a sense of what it will look like. (Carol laughs) Or rather, what it is supposed to look like.*

While it likely only takes a few minutes, a pre-observation meeting or Checkpoint Pre-briefing such as this one between observers and the teacher being observed is critical. Carol has clearly articulated the focus that would be most helpful to her and therefore provided a specific lens to look through for the observing team. By doing this, she has created safety for herself as the observed AND the observing team. They know Carol wants specific feedback in the three areas she outlined. She is not asking for observations about the wallpaper, the cleanliness of her room, or which students are behaving properly during the lesson—observations about these areas would be unsolicited and therefore inappropriate. Much like the restaurant we described in an earlier chapter, the "furniture and feels" are not what's important to Carol; it's the instructional "meal" she is serving and how that meal is received by her "customers."

As we shared previously, a useful thought when observing Checkpoints is to be the cameraperson, not the journalist. The objective of

Checkpoint Observations is not to create a narrative for the teacher based on the opinions of those doing the observations. Instead, we want observers to provide additional sets of eyes so the teacher can connect their culturize actions to the impact those actions had on their students. Observers are not there to judge; they are there to provide observations specific to the focus areas outlined by the teacher in the pre-meeting. Let's consider examples of journalistic, opinion-based observations and compare them to sample Checkpoint observations based on Carol's focus areas.

| Journalist Observations | Checkpoint Observations |
| --- | --- |
| *"Some of the students seemed disengaged."* | *"7 of 11 students I spoke to could tell me what they were doing and why it was important to them. 4 of 11 students had not yet started the task."* |
| *"The teacher did a good job conferencing with the students."* | *"After student group-teacher conferences, some students could move on to the next step in the activity. After individual student-teacher conferences, each student could move on to the next step in the activity."* |
| *"The students were familiar with the routines in the classroom"* | *"After the teacher gave instructions verbally and referred to anchor charts, 14 of 20 students started the task. 6 students sat quietly."* |

In the Journalist observations, you will notice language such as "seemed disengaged," "did a good job," and "the students were familiar." While these statements might have been true, they required judgment by the observer. A quick way to make the observations in the left column more observable is to ask ourselves, "What did I observe that made me think that?" This simple question helps us clarify our observations in a way that invites the person we are observing to reflect on the impact of their actions.

Consider the last pair of observations above. As a teacher being observed, which feedback would spur more reflection for you about practice and impact? If we say, "The students were familiar with routines in the classroom," much like putting a letter grade at the top of an essay for students, our judgment can inadvertently stop the reflection process. However, by specifically stating, "After the teacher gave instructions verbally and referred to anchor charts, 14 of 20 students started the task. Six students sat quietly," the observed teacher can now ponder a whole host of questions, such as, "I wonder what else I might do for those six students?" and "I wonder why that worked for those fourteen students?"

If we want our Checkpoint observations to lead to reflection on our practice, we must ensure they are specific and judgment-free. Remember, these observations are not an evaluation. Th y are an opportunity to learn with and from each other to culturize our classrooms.

Prior to entering Carol's classroom, Connie gave the team a few instructions. She had spoken to Principal Jennifer earlier in the week to get some ideas–Jennifer had already established herself as a school leader who provided useful feedback to teachers and teams. Connie had checked in with Jennifer to see if there were a few tips she could pass along to her teammates. Jennifer suggested three things, which Connie relayed to her team.

The first idea Connie shared was "Look down, listen up." Because there can be a tendency to focus on the teacher during observations,

Jennifer found it useful to "listen up" to what the teacher was saying, but "look down" to see what the students were doing as a result of what was said or what the task was actually requiring of the students. The second one was to be the cameraperson, not the journalist and make sure that the team acted as that additional set of eyes. Jennifer also found it helpful to have someone act as the statistician, a team member who counted the students in the classroom and ensured each observer was not spectating–that they were jotting down observations. Luis was perfect for this.

Now let's see what the team saw during their observation of Carol's Champion for Students-focused lesson in her Grade 5 Math class. Upon entering the classroom, Luis quickly counted 21 students in the class. Each team member stood or sat in different parts of the class, and a few students turned to wave at their visitors.

The class began with Carol saying, "OK friends, we are going to get this afternoon started with 'This or That.' But before we begin, I want to ensure we know what we are doing. On a scale from 1-5 with five being 'Teacher Carol, I've got this!' and one being 'Teacher Carol, I have no idea what you mean by 'This or That,' I want you to tell me how well you remember 'This or That' by writing 1, 2, 3, 4, or 5 on your whiteboard and holding it up high facing me so I can see it." Several class members giggled and wrote 1 on their whiteboard, but then changed their number to 5. Luis noted that 21 of 21 students wrote a 5 on their whiteboards–they had done this routine before.

Soon after, pictures began flashing on the projector screen showing similar products in two columns. One column was labeled "this" and the other "that." Students were to quickly determine the better deal by adding the products together. Once finished, they held up either a "this" or "that" sign to signal their answer. Connie noted that after each time the students made their thinking visible, Carol made a note in her planning book. Luis noted that each student answered on their whiteboard. Thomas observed that several students were getting the wrong answer.

After warming up for four or five minutes with "This or That," Carol drew the attention of the class to the learning standard that was displayed on the projector:

*"Reading and writing decimals to thousandths using base-ten numerals, number names, and expanded form."*

"Friends," Carol said, "at your tables with your group of three, I want you to brainstorm all the reasons why learning about reading and writing decimals might be important for us and a burning question that you might have. Then together, I want your table group to put your top three reasons why learning decimals might be important and that you think might excite other groups to learn about decimals on your group whiteboard. If you are not sure why they might be important, you can choose to ask a question instead. Each group member must contribute one reason or one question they might have. You will also ooo that I have written the directions here on the board in case you need to refer back to them."

Luis noted that 4 of the 7 groups started the task immediately, using content-specific dialogue to brainstorm ideas. Tamika leaned into one of the groups, and heard one student say, "I think decimals are important for when we buy shoes. My basketball shoes are size 7.5, and when I had size 7s, I got blisters." Connie noticed that while students were working in their triads, Carol quietly pulled four students aside for a short individual conference, pointing to her planning book while she chatted with them. Luis noticed that each student wrote either a reason why learning decimals was important or a question they had about decimals.

After five minutes, Carol had each group bring their team whiteboard up to the front to display in front of the classroom. She then had each student use their individual whiteboards to pick their favorite reason for learning about decimals from one of the other groups and to put a star next to a question at the front of the room generated by a different group they felt was important to be answered. The question with the most stars beside it was "What's better to use, decimals or fractions?"

Thomas saw that 2 of the 7 groups only had questions on their team whiteboard—they had not generated ideas about why decimals were important. He also noticed that each student was able to select one important reason for learning decimals and put a star beside one burning question. Tamika observed that the two reasons that appeared most often on individual whiteboards were "sports stats" and "knowing how much things cost." She smiled when she noted that "making sure your shoes fit" was a close third. The team watched Carol take a picture of the class and their whiteboards with her phone and say, "I'm getting old, friends. I need to take a picture so I can remember this for later." The class laughed.

Carol congratulated the class for all they knew about decimals and took time to respond to the most popular questions. She then asked the students to pull out their exit tickets with a problem from the previous day to begin a brief mini-lesson. Luis quickly counted that 8 of 21 students had their exit tickets in front of them. Carol then spent the next ten minutes working through the problem as a whole group. Thomas noticed that four students consistently put their hands up to answer questions that Carol was verbally posing to the whole group. He also observed that Carol frequently called on one of those four students after waiting for a short period for responses from other members of the class. It struck him that the other students were almost waiting for those four students to answer—they seemed to recognize that if they stayed silent, someone else would respond. Connie heard one student whisper, "When will we ever use this stuff?" to another member of her group just as the mini-lesson concluded.

Carol then asked the students to pull out the data project they had worked on the past few days. Students were able to choose their own data category; however, it had to include decimals to the hundredths place. Students had a set of data analysis questions they needed to answer, and they were to support why this particular piece of data was important to them. Students were also required to present their findings to a small group of peers in their class using a visual aid of their choice such as video, poster, or slide.

Thomas noticed that each student quickly pulled out their project, and two students waved him over to show him what they had been working on. They had created a map with all the gas stations within a ten-mile radius with the current gas prices over the last ten days. "They all raised gas prices on Tuesday, but then these stations dropped them back down on Thursday. These stations didn't," the students said with excitement. When Thomas asked them why they were so concerned about gas, he discovered that each of them had siblings who had recently gotten their drivers' licenses and were going to charge their younger siblings for gas. "I want to make sure my brother doesn't overcharge me!" said one of the students.

Tamika, Connie, and Luis noticed that, again, Carol had students at her desk doing small-group conferences. Two students were collecting data on the fastest 40-yard dash in NFL combine history, and Carol was highlighting the operations that the students used to chart their data using bar graphs. She encouraged the students when they wanted to include their own 40-yard dash times, and the students were excited to get their football coach to officially time them later in the week.

In the closing moments of the class, Carol did a whole group check-in during which students could choose to share a success or a struggle with the lesson, but had to jot down what their next step would be on an exit ticket. As the students were leaving, Carol collected the exit tickets, saying, "I noticed earlier that some of you might have 'accidentally misplaced' your exit tickets, so let me hang on to those for you, my friends." And with that, the class was dismissed. Carol quickly flipped through the exit tickets, and said, "Hmm, a number of these tickets tell me I need to revisit the whole group problem we did today. I think I missed the mark."

Connie and the team waited for the students to leave and then re-entered the classroom for a short debrief with Carol. They kept their comments about their observations focused on being a Champion for Students. At times, Carol could find herself overanalyzing everything, so she was grateful to get some immediate feedback from them so she would not be left to think about it over the weekend.

Each member of Connie's team thanked Carol and told her they looked forward to further debriefing with her after the weekend. "Off to soccer," Carol smiled, trotting down the hallway to head to the field with her team. Connie asked the team to keep their notes so they could unpack them as a group the next time they met.

Given the three things Carol wanted the team to notice and what happened in her class, what might be some specific, descriptive, and non-journalistic observations you could make about Carol's lesson to inform her practice in being a Champion for Students?

(i)   the different ways and how often students were able to show their learning

(ii)  if/when they could articulate why the concept was important to learn

(iii) what the students did as a result of the choices they were given

## PRESS PAUSE MOMENT: REFLECTION SPACE

◆

◆

◆

After a classroom observation, it's tempting for us to jump right in to what we liked, what we didn't like, and what we would have changed about the lesson. And if we are de-briefing with a teacher we have been observing, we often feel compelled to shower them with platitudes like, "Great lesson!" or, "I totally get why students love your class." We do want our colleagues to know we appreciate them having us into their classroom, but similar to our pre-observation approach, we want to ensure that we remember our role as cameraperson. Being focused on specific, descriptive observations about being a Champion for Students, Carrying the Banner, or whatever lens we have been given to look through in support of a teacher trying to culturize their classroom, is just as critical after the observation as it is before.

A key aspect of being a Champion for Students is getting to know the story of each student. In schools today, it's common to have student voice committees, leadership committees, Principals' advisory councils, and student surveys. However, a question we might ask ourselves is, "What are the observable changes that happen in the classroom as a result of us giving students 'voice'?"

If one were to ask if students have demonstrably changed in the last twenty years, we would hear a definitive, "Absolutely!" from the adults in our schools. However, if we asked ourselves if the styles of teaching and types of tasks and assessments have changed commensurately with the changes we see in our students (and we are being honest with ourselves), we might have to pause for thought. As much as a book report on *The Outsiders* might have been interesting for us adults back in the day, one must wonder when we see the same book (and perhaps digital book report format) today whether we are truly hitting the mark for kids. This is not to denigrate *The Outsiders* or any other literary classic, but rather for us to consider whether we are truly hearing our students and demonstrating we are listening to what they are saying by changing with them and for them.

Rather than trying to guess what is relevant and contextual to kids (which arguably can change in the span of a few upward swipes on their phones), it is vital we create the time to hear their individual voices and then demonstrate we've listened to them by providing authentic and differentiated choices based on what they've told us. Conferencing provides us with an opportunity to be a Champion for Students. Using what we've learned in those conferences to help them connect our content to their context tells students that we are being a champion for each of them.

Let's drop into the post-observation conversation between Carol, Connie and the rest of the team:

*Tamika: Carol, on behalf of the entire team, I wanted to thank you for allowing us to learn from and with you in your classroom. Being observed requires courage and vulnerability, and we appreciate your willingness to allow us to share your classroom.*

*Connie: Carol, you asked us to look through three lenses. First, the different ways and how often students were able to show their learning*
    *Second, if and when they could articulate why the concept you were teaching was important to learn, and third, what the students did as a result of the choices they were given. Does that sound like what we talked about?*

*Carol: Sure does. I'm glad you weren't looking at my messy desk.*

*Connie: Great. So, team, the observations we share today need to be specific, descriptive and related to these three points. Agreed? Let's get started. Who would like to begin?*

*Luis: The first thing I noticed is that you used a number of different methods to get the kids to show their learning in different ways. As soon as students came into the classroom, you started with a routine—I think it was called "This or That"—that you had used before, but right away did a check-in to see if students remembered it. When you did that, I noticed that all 21 students responded, and most of them were 5/5s. It really set the tone for the class.*

*Thomas: Each time you used the whiteboards, I noticed that every student gave some sort of response. And I saw you jotted down notes almost every time the students wrote something on their boards. Can you tell us more about your notes?*

*Carol: When they can show me what they're thinking like they do with whiteboards, I want them to know I'm paying attention to them. I just jot down a few names and check in with them. Sometimes they try to trick me, so the whiteboard is not foolproof—I still have to follow up with them.*

*Thomas: I was wondering about that—sometimes my students tell me they understand just so I will leave them alone (group laughs).*

*Carol: That's why I take pictures of their whiteboards—I can quickly look back and see if I have gotten to the students I need to. They think I have this amazing memory—do I ever have them fooled! But the camera and the notes help them know I care about whether they have learned it.*

*Connie: You had the 1 to 5 check, the whiteboards, the connections and burning questions activity, the dot activity where students showed which idea or question was important to them—there were numerous opportunities for students to show their learning. Would everyone agree that when students had the opportunity, they consistently made their thinking observable in different ways? (nods around the room)*

*Luis: In the second part of the lesson when the class was reviewing the problem that was done the previous day, I noticed that 8 out of 21 students had their exit tickets.*

*Carol: Wow, I didn't notice that so many hadn't brought them. I knew a few hadn't, but that's good intel.*

*Thomas: When the problem was being done on the whiteboard for the whole class and the questions were posed verbally to the group, four students consistently put their hands up to respond. The other students seemed to wait for those four.*

*Carol: That's something I want to work on. Sometimes I just want to get through those review problems, and those four kiddos are so eager. I wouldn't have noticed those other students sitting back and waiting.*

*Tamika: I found it interesting that when activities allowed students to show their thinking in different ways, each student responded. When the students were able to show their thinking in one way, four students responded.*

*Carol: OK, great point. That makes sense.*

If we examine the dialogue between Carol and the observation team, each of the observations mentioned by the team was related to the lens Carol had invited them to look through. Connie's norming of the group at the beginning of the conversation to be specific to Carol's look fors was instrumental and cannot be over-emphasized. As a result, the team stayed on point. Even when Luis, Thomas, and Tamika pointed out aspects of the second part of the lesson when four students were the predominant responders to questions, they made sure their language was related to the points they were asked to notice.

Words matter when it comes to Checkpoint observations, specifically when we are trying to be the cameraperson rather than the journalist. Consider this example of what Luis actually said as a cameraperson:

*Cameraperson Luis: In the second part of the lesson when the class was reviewing the problem that was done the previous day, I noticed that 8 out of 21 students had their exit tickets.*

Here is what Luis could have been tempted to say as a journalist:

*Journalist Luis: In the second part of the lesson, when the class was reviewing the problem that was done the previous day, I noticed that **only** 8 out of 21 students had their exit tickets.*

One word ("only") changes the tone of the statement, doesn't it? Eight students had their exit tickets—that's not good; that's not bad... it's eight. The person who needs to reflect on that number is Carol; perhaps the day before, two students brought their exit tickets, prompting her to think, "Hmmm, I wonder why today that number was eight?" Maybe the day before, nineteen students brought their exit tickets, prompting her to again think, "Hmmm, I wonder why today that number was eight?" In the end, Carol is the one who is assessing the teaching and learning in her classroom and how her actions to culturize the classroom impacted her students.

Let's rejoin the Checkpoint Debrief, which is getting close to wrapping up:

*Connie: Carol, during the activity when students had a choice in their data project, each of the students I chatted with was able to tell me what they were doing and why it was important to them.*

*Thomas: Two students were almost bursting trying to advise me where I should buy gas. One thing I noticed though was that you found ways to check in with your students at several different points during your lesson. And each time you checked in, I noticed that the student got right back to work.*

*Tamika: I saw that as well. I realize now that I can check in with my students more often. Carol, given all our observations, what patterns are emerging for you?*

*Carol: A couple, actually. First, when I gave students choice, more of them seemed to be able to tell you their "why." (Group nods) Second, when I gave students one way to demonstrate their learning, only a few students were willing to do so in that way. This is making me re-think the way I review questions in the classroom. The other thing I think I am hearing is that choice and check-ins are starting to make a difference. It's work, but It's worth it.*

*Luis: On behalf of our team, we appreciate you hosting us in your classroom. Carol, I hope that you can share some of the ideas that are working for you with the rest of the staff.*

It is important to note that a debriefing after a classroom visit can look different than what we described here. The time, length, process, and location can vary based on your current situation and team dynamics. However, we do recommend that you work towards a more formal, structured post-conference approach that is conducted periodically so that your conversations and connections as a cohesive unit become clearer, deeper, more reflective, and more impactful.

Whether it's Checkpoint observations, lesson analysis, or simply reflecting on our practice to culturize our classroom, we must ensure we connect what we try to what we want to see: our Culturize Checkpoints. Carol's "When...then..." statements allow her to link things like voice and choice to students' ability to tell her their why and build agency and efficacy. But connecting action to impact is not only powerful for self-reflection, it's also constructive when sharing impactful practices that have culturized our classrooms with others.

# CHAPTER 6

⌁

# Try. Learn.
# Share. Repeat.

*"There is no excuse not to try."*

—Barack Obama

Imagine arriving in a new city after a long afternoon flight, your stomach growling louder than the city traffic outside your hotel window. You reach for your phone, eager to uncover the culinary treasures awaiting you. A quick Google search reveals a number of dining options within a mere ten-minute stroll. Excitement builds as you anticipate the flavors and experiences that await.

However, your enthusiasm is quickly dampened as you delve into the many reviews. Instead of insightful critiques or glowing recommendations, you're met with a series of vague remarks. "It was OK," one reviewer nonchalantly remarks, while another simply states, "Fine, I guess." Frustration mounts as you continue scrolling, hoping for clarity amidst the ambiguity. Every restaurant claims to be one of the best, but you smile when you read those, as you've never heard of a restaurant that says, "We make average food."

Amidst the lukewarm sentiments, a beacon of hope emerges—a review declaring, "This place is awesome!" Yet, it's swiftly countered by a damning verdict of "Terrible." Conflicting opinions leave you at a loss, unsure of where to turn for reliable guidance. With a sigh of resignation, you reluctantly abandon your quest for food and resort to your go-to meal when you just need something quick—an old Clif bar in your backpack washed down with a cup of hotel decaf coffee. Navigating the gastronomic landscape of this new place without the benefit of reviews to guide you will have to wait for when you have more time.

But what would a helpful review look like? As someone new to the area, you likely want the review to be specific and descriptive about things like dishes, flavors, and price. You might want to know how difficult it is to get a reservation, parking, and access. If you have specific dietary needs or allergies, you might also want to know if there are flavorful eating options. Who is doing the reviewing may also be important; a businessperson looking for a quiet meal might have a different perspective than someone with young ones and looking for a child friendly menu. Ultimately, you want to know if the meal is worth the time and effort given all the other restaurant choices that are available, so a review saying, "It was amazing!" or "Didn't work for me." isn't going to help very much.

For educators, digging into the work of things such as equity, differentiation, student engagement, and the other big concepts that tend to be embedded in our vision statements can often feel like landing in a new city in search of a meal. We are hungry to meet the needs of our students, but we also appreciate guidance from those who have gone before us. Much like restaurants, each program or potential solution to our problem will advertise that it is the right choice for us. Not to mention, it seems that there is some form of research that supports nearly every perspective. As a result, one of our most compelling sources of validation tends to be our peers.

We want authentic reviews from educators and leaders who work hard like we do, who have students like our students, in schools like our schools. But too often in education those reviews are few and far between. We consume a lot of initiatives, but rather than regularly scheduled, specific, descriptive, and purposeful observations and sharing of the approaches that have impact in our classrooms, we tend to say things like, "We tried that once," or "Didn't work for me," and leave busy educators to try and figure it out on their own. It's little surprise that we sometimes fall back on our go to strategies and ideas when it comes to culturizing the classroom—we're just not sure if the return on effort is going to come out in our favor when trying things that are new or different. Cue the flattened Clif bar and decaf coffee—it's not the perfect meal, but it will get us through.

Culturizing the classroom is everyone's responsibility. While we cannot expect everyone to do everything all at once, as Barack Obama said, "There is no excuse not to try." However, with something as important as school culture, we must go further than just trying. Earlier in the book, we described a process to create observable Culturize Checkpoints. We detailed how we might then use those Checkpoints to assess our current state, narrow our focus, and determine one thing that we can implement in our context. But just trying one thing one time and then following it up with a review like, "That didn't work," or "It was OK" would be the surface-level skipping from initiative to initiative that happens far too often in our schools. Examining and changing culture is challenging and complex work, and the one and done approach is not enough.

When trying to culturize our classrooms, not everything we try will work. Not the first time. Not every time. And even when we happen upon those approaches that might have "unicorn" status, it's not just the strategy itself, it's the nuances of how we implement the strategy in our context. When we are doing the work of culturizing the classroom, we want to hear the magic—those tiny details from our peers that truly make the difference. There is individual conferencing, and there is the way you did individual conferencing that you noticed led to something significant in your students. That's the grit we want to hear about when we share with our peers. The same can be said regarding larger scale initiatives our profession is known for (think literacy and math) that seem to change every few years. When we label an initiative as "failing" we must reflect and ask ourselves, "Why did the initiative fail?"

> When we label an initiative as "failing" we must reflect and ask ourselves, "Why did the initiative fail?"

Was the initiative the issue or was it the *way* we implemented it that caused it to fail? We would argue that it is more often the latter. Process matters.

In truth, the Observable Impact model in culturizing our classrooms described to this point is not just designed to build the culture of a school. It is also designed to make it easier for educators and leaders to connect what they do around culture to the impact it has on kids. When we can more explicitly connect what we do to what we observe in our students (which can have a positive or negative impact), we can make practical, evidence-based decisions about which actions we need to amplify, elevate, and proliferate to culturize our classrooms. In short, when a strategy we try to positively change the culture in our schools does not work (or, more specifically, does not lead to what we want to observe in our students), we need to share that, too. There's nothing to be ashamed of; we are all trying our best.

Earlier in the book, we emphasized that culture is everyone's responsibility. If we truly believe this, then the design, implementation, sharing of strategies, and reflection upon strategies to culturize the classroom should not be left to one or two dedicated educators who are keen to share, or even a front-running, grade-level team. Everyone needs to own a part of the culture building process. Our words on the wall would never say, "Some of us are Champions for Students." Each individual needs to pull their weight if we want to reach the results for which we are aiming. As a result, it is vital to create structures that support all educators and hold us all laterally accountable, much like that running partner who bangs on our door at 5 a.m.

Let's check in on Connie and her team just prior to their Spring staff meeting:

*Thomas: So what's this that we have to share the stuff our team has been doing around culture?*

*Luis: This is what Jennifer said back in January, right Connie? I remember she wanted to give us plenty of notice–she said, "Circle this date on your calendar."*

*Thomas: (frowns) I don't remember that, but I might have missed something. Anyhow, Connie, are you OK to present for our group? You know this stuff upside down and backwards, and everyone loves you. You will be the star of the show.*

*Connie: I don't think that's an option. Jennifer told me she will be splitting us into vertical teams so we can hear different ideas and different perspectives from members of different groups. I actually think it's a great idea. I've heard about some pretty cool things that the other teams are trying.*

*Thomas: I don't know if I like that. I don't feel like I have much to share. And I hate those small group things. We will probably have to toss some yarn around and sing songs.*

*Connie: Thomas, you have been doing the work just like we have. Of course you can do this. The way you have implemented individual conferencing for your kids has been really cool, and you told me yourself that you were pretty excited about it.*

It's not uncommon for us to be nervous when sharing what we are doing in our classrooms—we are used to being behind closed doors. Even though educators present and share lessons with their students each day, it feels a bit different when we present and share with our colleagues. Splitting teacher teams into vertical groups or cross-content teams in which each group member gets to give and hear individual perspectives on the impact of strategies is useful for a variety of reasons:

- Small groups tend to be less intimidating for those who are sharing.
- Small groups increase chances for interactions, especially when augmented with protocols to ensure all voices are heard.
- Teams from different grade levels or content areas can provide different perspectives and applications.
- When the vertical groups disperse and reassemble in their grade-level or content area groups, they multiply the opportunity to bring back more ideas from different perspectives.
- When each individual has to share their experiences instead of one person acting as a representative for an entire team, each individual is held accountable for their actions to build school culture.

In the reflection space below, how might you design a faculty meeting or a PD Day where:

(i) each staff member shares the work they have done to culturize their classroom?

(ii)   each staff member gets to hear from other staff members?

(iii)  each staff member feels safe sharing successes and failures?

(iv)   each staff member takes away multiple strategies they can try in their classroom?

(v)    each member commits to trying at least one new thing to culturize their classroom as a result?

## PRESS PAUSE MOMENT: REFLECTION SPACE

+

+

+

Perhaps you designed a faculty meeting similar to Jennifer, who:

+ Pre-selected groups of four with representatives from different grade levels and subject areas.

+ Gave time for each group to describe what they had worked on to culturize their classroom, followed by a reflection protocol for the rest of the group.

+ Had each group member rotate as a presenter.

+ Had grade-level and subject-specific groups reassemble in a reconnection session after being in their pre-selected groups. This was to have teams reflect on strategies they had learned from other grade levels about culturizing their classrooms.

+ Had each team member fill out a digital exit ticket describing one strategy they would try to culturize their classrooms using what they had learned during the faculty meeting. She published these the following day so everyone could see what each team member would work on moving forward.

So how did this spring meeting go for Jennifer? The meeting started well enough. There were a few minor grumblings from a few staff members about having to sit in assigned groups, but this quickly abated when Tina (one of the teachers from the English department) laughed and said to the group, "We make the kids do this all the time, so I guess we can do this." To kick off the meeting, Jennifer gave a short list of norms to guide the sharing sessions, including "Be kind, be specific, and be helpful" and "Assume best intentions." Groups were then asked to assemble in different parts of the library and begin sharing their work to culturize their classrooms.

As Jennifer walked around the library, she noticed that some groups got right down to work. Luis was presenting the work that he and the rest of the Science department had undertaken to become Champions for Students through implementing individual conferencing to get to know their students and what was relevant to them. Luis's group was nodding intently and scribbling notes as he described how the department used what they had learned during the conferences to make their science content more relevant by connecting it to things that mattered to their students. Carol was describing how the Science team had visited her classroom and given her feedback about calling on the same students during Q and A time, and how she had changed her practice to be more inclusive of each student. Jennifer was swelling with pride.

However, as Jennifer listened in on each of the groups, she noticed a few things:

+ Many teachers appeared to have tried something to culturize their classroom. However, some had pictures of their students, student work samples, and even takeaways for other group members, while a number of teachers had little to share. One teacher had his arms crossed and was sitting four feet outside the group's circle.

- Some group members presented to their small group for 10-15 minutes while some group members shared for less than two minutes. As a result, some groups finished far earlier than others. This led to several side conversations. In one such conversation, Jennifer overheard three teachers saying, "I didn't know that we were all supposed to be as good as Carol at this stuff."

- The grade-level reconnection meetings after the vertical group sessions were positive—many teams indicated they learned several things from other teams that they could implement in their own classes.

- A few staff members did not fill out the exit ticket. One wrote, "Why do we have to do this stuff for culture? Can't I just teach my class?"

Overall, Jennifer had mixed feelings about the faculty meeting. Clearly, many teachers had leaned into creating a more positive culture in their classrooms and she felt good about this. They were taking the work of culturizing their classrooms seriously and shared evidence of the work they had done with their colleagues.

However, Jennifer was still bothered by the lack of effort put forth by some of her teachers to change the culture of their classrooms. These were some of the same people who were most vocal when complaining about the culture of the school. And now they were silent when asked to share what they were doing about it? This was frustrating for Jennifer. She had tried to create an experience for her teachers that would allow them to learn from each other. To learn with each other. Now she just felt deflated. Was this work to move from words on the wall to classroom impact really worth it?

For many leaders, moments like these, when our first efforts to move the needle on something so important as culture don't go according to plan, can be discouraging. We know that developing a positive culture is critical. Yet it seems like when we try to do something about it, we are met with resistance, apathy, or both. Not from everyone, but from enough to make us question ourselves and our efforts.

At the beginning of the book, we describe the trepidation and uncertainty that confronted Brooks when he was finally paroled from Shawshank Prison after years of incarceration. When it comes to moving from words on the wall to classroom impact, leaders must be prepared to encounter these "Brooks moments" of self-doubt, wondering whether it's all worth it and considering a return to what we have done before. For Brooks, these moments of uncertainty became too overwhelming for him to handle on his own. This is the key piece we can learn from Brooks's situation in *The Shawshank Redemption*—he was trying to navigate a significant change by himself without any support, leading him to succumb to the pressures of dealing with change on his own. Similarly, a leader cannot drive the work of culturizing the classroom by themselves; they need the support of their office team, leadership team, and the entire staff. In the next chapter, let's consider how we might begin to layer support in a way that builds capacity, momentum, and efficacy.

CHAPTER 7

~

# Decreasing the Distance: Layering Change

*"Design is really an act of communication, which means having a deep understanding of the person with whom the designer is communicating with."*

–Don Norman, Author of *The Design of Everyday Things*

*J*ennifer sat in her office at the end of a long day reflecting on what had transpired with her staff over the past year. This was not how she had envisioned the year ending. The energy and excitement she felt previously had all but vanished. At the spring staff meeting, she watched many of her staff members take significant strides forward in moving their work to culturize their classroom from words on the wall to tangible strategies and approaches in their classrooms. And yesterday, she had prepared what she thought was a strong farewell message that acknowledged both the progress they had made in reimagining the culture of their school and the necessary next steps the staff would need to take to continue their work in creating a positive culture at the school. Where did things go wrong?

She had put together a PowerPoint presentation showing data on student attendance, office referrals, and state testing results, highlighting the successes and shortcomings of the year. She applauded their efforts and told them she appreciated them. But her words quickly fell flat when she shared that she needed them to take a deeper look at what they could do differently in their classrooms next year.

"We need to do a better job of reaching all students," Jennifer stated. "We have too many disengaged students and we saw an increase in office referrals. Although we saw a slight improvement in our attendance, our overall scores dipped slightly. In the coming weeks, I will work on the School Improvement Plan and have it ready to go for the start of next year."

The room fell silent. The smiles and laughter which had radiated the room over the last few months were no longer visible, having been replaced by a more somber mood. Grumblings could be heard throughout the room, with some teachers showing their frustrations.

To say Jennifer was disappointed would be an understatement. She was heartbroken and at a loss for what to do next. She had always prided herself on being a positive person. While some might see the glass as half empty or half full, Jennifer saw the glass as simply needing a refill, but now she felt completely drained. For the first time in her career, a cloud of self-doubt loomed over her as she sat alone in her office.

The next morning, feeling drained after an emotional evening reflecting on the faculty meeting and the comments made by some teachers, Jennifer decided to stop by Connie's classroom to get her take on the way things had gone this year. As one of the members of her inner circle, she respected Connie and trusted that Connie would be straight with her. Connie shared with Jennifer that she had come across a little tone-deaf in her comments. Many staff members had been working hard to improve the culture in their classrooms, but Connie felt Jennifer didn't acknowledge the specific actions that people had taken in the classroom. Connie pointed out that the staff had spent a great deal of time and effort creating their Culturize Checkpoints, but Jennifer had failed to mention a single one of them.

Jennifer was stunned. She tried to defend her actions at the staff meeting and blame the perceptions of the current culture of the school on a few individual teachers, but when she did, Connie had to interject.

"Jennifer, if I am hearing you right," stated Connie, "you are frustrated by some teacher's comments about not being able to reach some students because they won't do the work, but, respectfully, not only did you forget to acknowledge the work that had been done, aren't you doing the same thing by saying that you can't improve the morale of those teachers because they refuse to try? How is that any different?"

Jennifer processed the question before responding. "That's different Connie. We are talking about adults versus kids. They should know better."

Their conversation continued for an hour or so and when their time together ended, they thanked one another for taking the time to listen to what each had to say. "One final thought before you leave, Jennifer. You asked me why some staff don't seem to trust the administration. I think it's because some people perceive that decisions are made without ever asking us our thoughts. Many of us were already here when you started here. They have a lot of history and valuable insights they could offer. I think they resent the fact that no one ever asks them. That might be something for you to consider."

As Jennifer left the room, she turned around and said, "Thank you for your thoughts, Connie. I appreciate it."

But therein lies the challenge with change—when the distance between those who are driving the change and those who are implementing the change increases, so does the likelihood of us hearing things like, "Why are we doing this?" "Where is this coming from?" and "Why didn't they ask us?"

Change can be hard for those who are driving the changes AND for those who have to implement the change. But therein lies the challenge with change—when the distance between those who are driving the change and those who are implementing the change increases, so does the likelihood of us hearing things like, "Why are we doing this?" "Where is this coming from?" and "Why didn't they ask us?"

In the reflection space below, think of a time when you were resistant to change in your context.

(i)   What was the change?

(ii)  What were some of the reasons you resisted?

(iii) What was the outcome in terms of results?

(iv)  What could have been done differently that would have helped you be more accepting of the change?

(v)   What did you learn about yourself in that situation? What did you learn about the change process?

## PRESS PAUSE MOMENT: REFLECTION SPACE

♦

♦

♦

While it may have become a cliche to say, "The only constant we have is change" it's also not far from the truth. There will always be changes that come at us in our schools—new initiatives, new curriculum, new staff members, new leaders, and new kids. During the pandemic, new variables were thrown at schools on a near-daily basis resulting in an all-time high in change fatigue for educators in the school system. Unsurprisingly during this time, leaders felt reluctant to ask teachers to do even one more thing, fearing that the weight of the slightest additional snowflake of change could lead to an avalanche of negative responses from their staff. In the spirit of preserving well-being and compassion for busy teachers, it was not uncommon for leaders to make more decisions in the absence of those who would be required to bring those changes to life in the classroom. In other words, leaders sometimes increased the distance between those who were making decisions about change and those who would be required to implement those changes.

In *The Learning Leader: How to Focus School Improvement for Better Results*, Douglas Reeves writes:

*"Distributed leadership is based on trust, as well as the certain knowledge that no single leader possesses the knowledge, skills, and talent to lead an organization..." (2006, page 28).*

Deep down, like many leaders, Jennifer knew she could not do it all on her own. When it comes to the work schools do around things such as culture, engagement, equity, literacy, inclusion, and other school initiatives, no individual can make significant and sustainable changes in these areas by doing the work themselves, yet many leaders still feel overwhelmed and at times unsure what to do. Why? For one, these issues are complex and not simple to resolve. They are deeply layered in strong beliefs, varied skill sets, and personal biases and experiences. Two, leaders ultimately feel (and at times are held) responsible for finding a solution and in their desire to "fix" the issues, react quickly and move forward with a plan that has not been co-created with staff. And three, although co-creating seems like a logical approach, having the entire staff jump into the work of change can be unwieldy and cause all sorts of consternation among those responsible for leading change, especially in the early stages.

Earlier in the book, Jennifer told Connie that she wanted to change her approach as a leader. Learning from her time as an assistant principal at her previous school, Jennifer saw the impact of a principal who took a less collaborative and more top-down approach to leadership. This was similar to what Connie and the rest of the staff experienced last year, and in many ways had brought Connie and Jennifer closer together. However, there is a trap that leaders can sometimes easily and unknowingly fall into when attempting to be more collaborative—the creation of "favorites" or the "inner circle" among staff members.

When it comes to solving school-wide problems or implementing new initiatives at scale, it is not uncommon for school leaders to assemble key players, a critical mass, or a guiding coalition to forge the trail and make it easier for the rest of the staff to follow along. However, there are a few points of caution when determining the makeup of these trailblazing teams. First, if being part of these groups is seen as an exclusive club requiring some special connection to the leader, that "buy in" or investment we were seeking from staff can quickly turn to growing numbers of individuals who become "bought out." These individuals don't feel they are part of "The Club," even though they might have ideas that could prove beneficial and impact the thinking in ways not previously considered by the lead group. We often label these folks with terms like "resisters," or "fundamentalists," neither of which are productive. Look back at the reflection space when you resisted an idea—would it help you get onboard if someone labeled you as a "resister"?

Second, if the makeup of these groups is simply based on personal relationships or position (friends, department chairs, grade-level leaders, lead teachers, administrators), we are also potentially limiting the skill sets, perspectives, experiences, and possibilities that could help us make more informed decisions and increase our critical mass.

This is not to say that either of these group formats are right or wrong; however, we must be aware of the unintended outcomes that might come along with them. When we create (either purposefully or unwittingly) an inner circle:

- we may build resentment among staff who aren't part of the "in" crowd.
- the skill set of the group may not be best-fit for the task.
- we can create an echo chamber that becomes more about affirmation and less about critical feedback.
- we limit the ability to build capacity among other staff members.
- we burn out the people we cannot afford to burn out.

Strategic leaders are effective leaders. They are not manipulative, but transparent and clear in their explanations so that others do not create a false narrative. They are cognizant that in their efforts to be *inclusive* they can inadvertently be *exclusive* of the people, perspectives, experiences, and skills they might need most to move forward in their context, so they make sure to avoid such pitfalls.

Simply put, when we are going somewhere new, our goal is for everyone to be clear about where we are going and how we plan to get there. While we are traveling, it is nice to have more leaders to help guide the journey and it is energizing to have highly motivated people who are excited and want to be with us on the trip. But if our van breaks down on the side of the highway, it's also nice when we have a mechanic—even if they might be a bit resistant from time to time. Being mindful of the skills required to help get us where we want to go and being inclusive in terms of giving those who might have the necessary skills, will get us farther along the journey, and, more importantly, get us there safely. Conversely, creating an exclusive inner circle often leaves us complaining when we're stuck on the side of the road and placing blame on those who we didn't really invite in the first place. In Jennifer's case, what she discovered is that while she pledged to Connie that she was going to be more collaborative and inclusive, she didn't quite get there. She connected with a few staff members she was close to, but that was it. In other words, she ended up complaining when her plan was stuck on the side of the highway and blaming educators who she really hadn't invited to be part of the process—ultimately causing damage to the morale in her building.

Why does this happen? Part of the reason is rooted in a common question we hear from leaders when we discuss the pitfalls of creating inner circles: "What if I create a diverse group, but they come up with something that I don't agree with as a leader?" This is a great question and a primary reason why leaders often find themselves making decisions in isolation.

Being a collaborative leader does not mean that the leader doesn't have a say in setting the direction for the group. It means we need to reframe our thinking and act more strategically in the way we implement change by examining our processes. Oftentimes, leaders find themselves wanting or having to make a change or implement a new initiative. This is when leaders are most vulnerable. If and when you find yourself in this situation—because you will—we have found that leaders are likely to have greater success when they ease into the change by layering the change. Consider the following scenario:

*John, a school principal, announces to his faculty that the administration will be utilizing a new walk-through tool focusing on student engagement. Expecting pushback from certain members of his faculty, he is relieved when the room falls silent when he asks if anyone has any follow up questions. A few days later, he finds out there are many questions and concerns about the tool. Weeks later he learns that some of his team leaders have been complaining that they feel they are being blamed for students' unwillingness to work. Finally, he learns that one of his assistant principals has made modifications to the tool that he feels aligns more with his own philosophy.*

It is not uncommon for district and building leaders to find themselves in similar experiences as the one described above. Many of us have encountered moments when we did our best to implement a change, but the change initiative did not yield the results we were hoping to get. John's story is similar to Jennifer's story described earlier in the chapter. Like Jennifer, his first efforts to improve student engagement, something he believed would help both teachers and students, did not go how he had hoped. What can we take away from both of their experiences? The reason they did not get the results they wanted was because they moved too quickly through the process, and, in doing so, increased the distance between themselves and those who eventually would be impacted the most by the change. They needed to layer the change process.

**Layering the Process:** Let's take a moment to examine the steps taken by both Jennifer and John during their quest to implement change in their buildings and see what we can take from their experiences. See if you can identify in the *pre-layer* and *layer* sections below what steps they took and which ones they may have left out that caused them to fall short of the outcomes they were hoping for.

Pre-Layer:

1. **Vision:** Leaders must be able to articulate a clear vision of what they hope to accomplish and why it is important. When we are not clear from the onset, we open ourselves up to others creating their own narrative of why we are doing what we are doing and often that narrative results in a negative perception.
2. **Voice:** Once the vision has been clearly shared, it is always a better practice to seek input from those who are most impacted by the change. Be sure to explain why you are seeking input and what you plan to do with the feedback. This is where leaders must identify and communicate before starting the process, clearly articulating the things they expect to happen because of this change.

3.  **Act:** Our notebooks and word documents are filled with notes we have taken, but if we do nothing with the information we have collected via interviews, surveys, tabletalks, meetings, workshops, etc., we risk losing credibility as leaders for wasting people's time or, worse yet, labeled as one who is unable or afraid to make the changes needed to improve the current conditions.

The first exposure to any new change is critical. Any mistake we make during the initial launch can quickly land us in recovery mode which is why change is often exhausting. One common mistake we see occur is when initiatives are shared out in large groups first. We believe this opens us up to potential issues; therefore, we feel it is necessary to be more strategic. By strategic, we mean we must be transparent and honest. Here are three steps we recommend to get started on the right foot:

Layer:

4.  **Inner Layer:** It is crucial that leaders make sure that their administrative team is in tune with their vision and their why. We see this team as one and that one needs to function as a high-performing team and be in unified agreement with the vision. There cannot be any broken links in the administrative or office team.

5.  **Middle Layer:** Every school leader needs a building leadership team to assist and guide them in leading the school. We must be clear in identifying their roles and responsibilities and clear in our expectations for implementing change. Rather than go straight to the entire staff to implement a new change, we recommend starting with a smaller Building Leadership

Team (BLT) to help build a more strategic process for implementing the change so we can experience success early on by working through potential hiccups. These early connections also allow us to build trust and confidence among people so they feel capable that they can support their team members by replicating the same processes with their smaller grade-level or department teams. It is important to note that growing the capacity of others is a crucial step in scaffolding change. One thing we know for sure is that if we cannot get our building leadership teams to effectively implement a change, then making that change happen with fidelity across the entire staff is highly unlikely.

6.  **Outer Layer:** Once the first two layers have been initiated, it is time to go to the masses—the entire staff. Please note that an effective process would have included BLT members effectively sharing information from the beginning and throughout the process with their teammates as well as information consistently flowing from the administration. Again, we never want to create a culture in which people are creating their own narrative due to our lack of communication. During this layer, BLT members serve as facilitators in their small group teams and together, as an entire staff, we seek input from those most affected by the change—and in most cases, that includes everyone.

When reading these last few paragraphs, we can sometimes catch ourselves saying, "Ugh, we don't have time to do this." However, when it comes to time, a question we might ask ourselves is, "How would we rather *spend* our time?" Working together with our fellow leaders, educators, students, and community to proactively determine challenges, brainstorm ideas, prototype solutions, and share how things went tend to be the things that fill our buckets as educational leaders. In a given situation, this might entail some pre-planning, a few meetings and several hours here and there. But with more eyes on the challenge and more brainpower working on the solution, this front-end time is much more likely to surface a human-centered solution that works for everyone. Conversely, when we make the choice not to involve those who will use the solution, the odds of creating a positive experience for people who are never involved in the solution are low, and the odds that we have developed any capacity for our community to help us solve future problems is zero. In all likelihood we will spend inordinate amounts of time dealing with repercussions down the road. Typically, this back-end time tends to be mired with confusion, complaints, resentment, and questions like, "Why didn't you just ask us?" Whether it's front-end time or back-end time, it's still time—the front end just seems immeasurably more pleasant.

By slowing down and spending more time layering the process on the front end, we believe you will experience greater success not only in making positive change, but also improving morale. When leadership is strategic and intentional, working with all staff members rather than in isolation or with a select few, we are able to see a greater impact—the impact that both Jennifer and John were hoping to see.

**A Deeper Dive into Decision Making:** In the true spirit of collaboration and transparency, it is vital for the leader to ensure that a Building Leadership Team (or any group, for that matter) knows what their role is in the decision-making process prior to starting the work. A useful way to approach this with a BLT is to use a publicly-shared, decision-making matrix, that might look something like this:

| | Level 1 | Decisions that are **made for us** (State, District, Mother Nature) |
|---|---|---|
| **Decisions** | Level 2 | Decisions that **I need to make** (Funding, Evaluations, Personnel Issues) |
| | Level 3 | Decisions that **I need to make with your thoughts, ideas and input** |
| | Level 4 | Decisions that **I want us to make together** |
| | Level 5 | Decisions **I want you to make** as a group |

Even school administrators don't get to make certain decisions. State-wide mandates, district-level initiatives, and snowstorms are just a few that are beyond our control as building leaders. These are Level 1 decisions, and as an BLT, while we could debate the latest state policy on the new ELA curriculum, we just need to get it done. Conversely, there are many other decisions about which an administrator might say, "I am happy for our team to make this decision and design this project as long as it aligns with our School Improvement Plan and with our agreements on what is best for kids." Level 5 decisions such as these give the BLT flexibility and choice.

Level 3 decisions can be a bit more involved. For example, a school leader may provide their vision and some design parameters for a particular project. Let's take the faculty meeting example from earlier in the book. The administrator might say:

"My current thinking is that I need your help. I want to design a staff meeting where:

(i)   *each staff member shares the work they have done to culturize their classroom.*

(ii)  *each staff member gets to hear from other staff members.*

(iii) *each staff member feels safe sharing successes and failures.*

(iv)  *each staff member takes away multiple strategies they can try in their classroom.*

(v)   *each member commits to trying at least one new thing to culturize their classroom as a result.*

*I want to characterize this a Level 3 decision: I am excited to hear your thoughts and ideas, and I believe as a BLT, we can make this better. However, it is important to me that each staff member shares their work and feels safe doing so."*

In this way, the leader has clearly communicated some specific outputs that they need from the group. By having a process such as this, the leader can still create a diverse and inclusive BLT with varied skills, perspectives, and ideas while ensuring their values and ideals are reflected in the work of the team.

Moreover, when district leaders clearly identify, explain, and model processes like the one shared throughout this chapter with principals and teachers, the more likely principals and teachers will use similar processes in their buildings and classrooms with staff and students. Superintendents and principals must be clear in their explanations, and communications. They must model effective practices alongside their principals and assistant principals respectively, so moving forward they can decrease the distance between themselves and those they serve. By layering their processes and creating these experiences for their teams, not only will they influence the next generation of district and school leaders to actually live the words on the wall, but they will also be able to see the positive impact their behavior can have on an entire school's culture.

# PRESS PAUSE MOMENT: REFLECTION SPACE

♦

♦

♦

# CONCLUSION

~

# Bringing it All Together

*"Opportunity is missed by most people because
it is dressed in overalls and looks like work."*

–Thomas Edison

Creating a positive school culture is an intricate, multi-layered process that demands thoughtful planning, genuine collaboration, persistent effort, and constant reflection. As educators and leaders, we often grapple with the challenge of instilling a vibrant, supportive, and effective learning environment amidst a myriad of responsibilities that come with our roles. We have tried to provide a pathway towards achieving a positive culture–a through line that allows us to not only see what a culturized classroom would lead to for our students, but also the role we play as educators, leaders, and the larger school community in making it happen. Culture is NOT a fluke: it is an opportunity in disguise and if we truly want to create a culture that has impact we can actually observe in the classroom, we all need to be in it together.

Throughout this book, we wanted to put the work into a context that might resonate with educators. And while it might not be identical to your situation, we hoped you might relate to some of the fictitious characters in the story interwoven throughout this book. Jennifer, the bright new principal with big ideas doing her best to become a more collaborative leader but realizing that collaboration goes beyond working with the willing. Connie, the hard-working, honest teacher who truly wants what's best for her school and her students but gets frustrated by leadership forgetting that teachers are the ones who are asked to carry the biggest load, yet always seem to have the smallest voice. The eclectic collaborative team, with a cast of characters whose levels of skill and will to work on culture are as diverse as the students we teach in our schools (Each of us has encountered or maybe even at times may have been the "doubting Thomas"). The behind-closed-doors conversations with the eager and well-meaning school leader to let them know we DO support their ideas, but helping them understand that when they get too far ahead, they leave the rest of us behind even if it is the right thing to do. The staff meeting that goes awry, despite our planning and best intentions. The rueful shakes of our heads when we try something new as a leader or a teacher and it falls flat on its face. In truth, working on building a positive culture in a school is a non-linear process in the best of times, and we hope that the story part of the book would help all of us realize that the struggle is real, getting started is key, and DOING is the goal not PERFECTION.

In terms of getting started, at this point you might be saying, "Hey, wait a minute. They only covered ONE of the Core Principles. What about the other three?" Please know this is deliberate—this is that fine line we spoke of earlier in the book between showing and telling. We wanted to provide a framework for educators and leaders to unpack the Core Principles in a way that makes sense in their context. Specifically, for each Core Principle, we want schools to:

1. **Co-create their Culturize Checkpoints** beginning with what each Core Principle would LEAD TO for their students to

drive what teaching, tasks, and leadership LOOK like. Ensuring Checkpoints are observable by subjecting them to the Teenager Test, the Civilian Test, and the New Teacher Test we make it easier for ourselves to actually see them when they are happening in our classrooms.

2.  **Use their Culturize Checkpoints** to determine where they are at and where they want and need to go next. Determining whether we observe these Checkpoints consistently, sometimes, or not yet is critical, but not as a passing or failing grade. Instead, doing an initial formative assessment allows us to design the next moves we make in a way that resonates for you in your context.

3.  **Start small** by selecting ONE of the Core Principles, even ONE aspect of ONE core principle. Respecting the idea that educators and leaders are busy while simultaneously recognizing that culture is everyone's responsibility, and the difference between "nothing" and "something" is ONE thing. We cause culture—it's not a fluke or something we can hope will happen.

4.  **Connect specific actions to specific Checkpoints** When trying things like providing choice, using tasks with varied entry points, individual conferencing in our classrooms, or even doing Checkpoint observations, avoid saying things like "Individual conferencing is really effective" or "the kids like when they have choices" or "creating tasks with varied points is hard" Instead, try saying, "When I used individual conferences...then I noticed students were consistently able to tell us what they were doing, why they were doing it, and how it connects to their context."

5.  **Share** Culturizing the classroom is a lot of work when individuals try to do it on their own. While each of us might only be working on ONE thing, when all of us are working on SOMETHING, it amounts to a lot of things. By scheduling regular

opportunities for educators and leaders to learn from each other, we not only lighten the load for each of us, but we also hold ourselves accountable to creating the culture each of us wants in our classrooms. Regular classroom visits and regularly scheduled staff-wide, small-group Culturizing the Classroom Celebrations signal that our culture is something we work on, not wish for. (Plus, these celebrations BUILD culture!)

Creating a positive culture in a school is challenging work. At a time when the most precious commodity busy educators and leaders have is time itself, asking each of us to spend more time on something like culture can seem daunting. Moreover, there will be moments when it will be tempting to go back to what we have always done, giving in to the pressures that come with new initiatives, new programs, new curriculum, new staff, and new leadership. We may find ourselves saying things like, "We don't have time to work on culture!" and after reading this book, we hope you realize that you are right, we don't have time to work on something as big as culture all by ourselves. Like Brooks found when he left Shawshank, even when we know change is a good thing, it doesn't mean it's easy and, more importantly, we can't do it alone.

If we are willing to do the work to co-create an observable vision for positive culture in our schools through the 4 Core Principles of Culturize and use it to assess where we are at, we can differentiate for ourselves and take small steps in a way that makes sense for each person in our organization. We believe that each of us has a role in developing that ideal culture in our schools, and we need to hold ourselves laterally accountable for doing the work we know we need to do. And when we break culture down into smaller parts in our classrooms and our schools and share the impact of our collective actions related to the four Core Principles of *Culturize*, we will see that we are better when we include everyone in the process.

In closing, *Words on the Wall* is our way of reminding all educators, regardless of title or role, to pay closer attention to the *behaviors* in our schools and determine whether they match the *words* printed on signs, walls, and posters throughout the campus. When our actions reflect those words, we not only protect them from losing their meaning, but also see the impact they have on the overall climate and culture of our school communities.

> When our actions reflect those words, we not only protect them from losing their meaning, but also see the impact they have on the overall climate and culture of our school communities.

As teachers and leaders, you know the importance of a positive culture and the impact it can have on every student and every staff member. Having said that, our vision for observable impact was never to restrict the leader to focus solely on the four Core Principles of *Culturize*, but rather the values that YOU and YOUR campus hold dear to who you aspire to be. You know your students, your staff, your community, your culture, and your current reality more than we ever will. So if you decide to focus your look-fors on literacy, engagement, inclusion, numeracy, personalized learning, relationships, or any other aspirations that adorn your walls and are considered big drivers in any school, we say go for it! Regardless of the "words" you aspire for, recognize there will be times you may find yourself feeling overwhelmed by all the things that you are expected to be good at. However, imagine your impact when you take these other "words" you value and, together as a collective group just like Jennifer and Connie did, you:

- Co-create specific Checkpoints you want to see in your classrooms, offices, hallways, and throughout the building.

- Use your co-created Checkpoints to determine where you are at and the next steps that make sense for all of you.
- Start small, but start together, and be that supportive training partner for each other.
- Ensure that you don't just say, "We tried that once," but determine the role you play by connecting your actions to the impact they had on your students and your culture.
- Share your work in a way that allows you to learn from each other.

We would never profess that our words above will solve all the challenges you face in your daily work, but we will profess that your impact will be greater when you are strategic in your approach and bring clarity to what the words on the wall will not only look like, but what they can lead to–a better version of you.

We hope that the words in this book will energize you and give you the confidence to take ANY concept and break it down into small, manageable steps that meet busy educators where they are and move them forward while allowing them to build efficacy and agency in the process. And when you do it in a way that causes everyone to build culture by moving from *Words on the Wall* to *observable impact*, you will see your impact where it matters most: In our classrooms and our schools, with our students and our educators.

# References

Birk, C. A. & McDowell, M. (2023). *Navigating Leadership Drift - Observable Impact on Rigorous Learning*. First Educational Resources.

Birk, C. A. & Larson, G. L. (2019). *PLC 2.0 - Collaborating for Observable Impact in Today's Schools*. First Educational Resources.

*Businessweek - Bloomberg*. Bloomberg.com. (2008, July 24). http://www.businessweek.com/business_at_work/time_management/archives/2008/07/continuous_part.html

Casas, J. (2017). *Culturize: Every Student. Every Day. Whatever It Takes*. Dave Burgess Consulting, Inc.

Casas, J. (2022). Recalibrate the Culture, ConnectEDD, Publishing.

City, E., Elmore, R., Fiarman, S., & Teitel, L. (2009). *Instructional rounds in education: A network approach to improving teaching and learning*. Harvard Education Press.

Halim, S, Wahid, R. and Halim, T. (2018). CLASSROOM OBSERVATION- A POWERFUL TOOL FOR CONTINUOUS PROFESSIONAL DEVELOPMENT (CPD). International Journal on Language, Research and Education Studies. 2. 162-168. 10.30575/2017/IJLRES-2018050801.

Reeves, D.B. (2006) *The Learning Leader: How to Focus School Improvement for Better Results, 2nd Edition*. ASCD.

Visible Learning MetaX (2023). Visible Learning. https://www.visiblelearningmetax.com/influences/view/cognitive_task_analysis

~

# Core Principle Culturize Checkpoint Samples

## CHAMPION FOR STUDENTS

Never quit on a student. When a student doesn't meet your expectations, **invest more time to understand their story**. Show compassion and empathy. When we take time to connect to their experiences, it shows we value them and their voice.

| At our school, you will see each of us being Champions for Students when… | | | |
| --- | --- | --- | --- |
| Our Students are… | Our Educators… | Classroom Tasks/ Assessments ••• | Our Leaders are… |
| S1. Sharing their thinking and understanding in different ways, through discussions, writing, presentations, or using technology. | E1. Use various ways to provide students a choice in how they demonstrate their understanding and thinking. | T1. Allow students to show their learning in more than one way; choice boards; digital student portfolios; presentation-based assessments. | L1. Researching and modeling ways to provide choice during staff learning events (staff meetings/ PD days) and creating protocols/ structures for teachers to try and share them with their colleagues. |

| At our school, you will see each of us being Champions for Students when… | | | |
|---|---|---|---|
| Our Students are… | Our Educators… | Classroom Tasks/ Assessments … | Our Leaders are… |
| S2. Telling us what they are doing, why it's important, and how it connects to their lives and experiences. | E2.Give pre-assessments and use ongoing individual conferences and formative assessments to understand what students know, their concerns, interests, and perspectives and apply them to their content. | T2. Have varied entry points and high exit points; tasks designed with evidence of a connection to student context; assessments that require students to make a claim and support it with evidence, and a personal connection. | L2. Modeling ongoing individual conferences and formative assessment techniques to understand teachers' concerns, interests, and perspectives so the leader can connect the learning to their staff. |

| At our school, you will see each of us being Champions for Students when... | | | |
|---|---|---|---|
| Our Students are... | Our Educators... | Classroom Tasks/ Assessments ... | Our Leaders are... |
| S3. Explaining why it's important for them to complete their work, try it multiple times even if it's hard, and different strategies to help themselves and others be successful. | E3. Work with students to co-create an understanding of the importance of tasks and contexts and model different ways to solve problems. | T3. Are multi-step tasks connected to issues that matter to students and their community; assessments that require students to apply multiple problem-solving methods to address an issue that is relevant to their context. | L3. Working with staff to analyze classroom tasks to ensure they are connected to students and help students to solve problems that are important to them and connected to their context. |

## EXPECT EXCELLENCE

What we model is what we get. **Model the behaviors you want others to emulate.** We should never ask others to do what we are not willing to do ourselves. Every school has average, but the best schools do not allow average to become the standard.

| At our school, you will see each of us 'Expecting Excellence' when... | | | |
|---|---|---|---|
| Our Students are... | Our Educators are... | Our Tasks... | Our Leaders... |
| S1. Comparing their work to success criteria to determine areas of strength, growth and next steps. | E1. Co-creating success criteria with students and using them to provide timely and specific feedback (both teacher and peer feedback). | T1. Allow students to make multiple attempts/do multiple drafts that show they have used feedback to meet criteria (IE. Bump-Up Boards, Peer Feedback Triads). | L1. Modeling the co-creation of success criteria with staff on school-based items/ structures (i.e. PT conferences, school policies) that support teachers co-creating criteria in their classes. |

| At our school, you will see each of us 'Expecting Excellence' when… | | | |
|---|---|---|---|
| **Our Students are…** | **Our Educators are…** | **Our Tasks…** | **Our Leaders…** |
| S2. Setting and meeting learning goals that help them meet important deadlines in class. | E2. Conferencing with students to help them create and monitor meaningful learning goals and access support for them to be successful. | T2. Are broken down into smaller steps and lead to goals that are meaningful to individual student context. | L2. Co-creating meaningful improvement plan goals with staff and breaking them down into small steps and ongoing checkpoints. |
| S3. Can clarify the challenge they are having, what they have tried and supports that might help them solve the problem. | E3. (Co) creating routines and protocols that help students name their problems and access different individual, peer and teacher supports (IE. sentence stems, task flow charts.) | T3. Are designed to help students learn to use different supports and describe why they chose that support to solve their problem. | L3. Developing protocols with educators to help them clarify classroom challenges and find practical solutions for their classrooms. |

## CARRY THE BANNER

Be a positive voice at all times for your students, colleagues, and families. Do your best to **create meaningful experiences** with those whom you come in contact with so when they walk away, they speak positively about their interaction with you.

| At our school, you will see each of us 'Carrying the Banner' when... | | | |
|---|---|---|---|
| Our Students are... | Our Educators are... | Our Tasks... | Our Leaders... |
| S1. Demonstrating active listening by using language that connects to the ideas of others or providing specific feedback or ideas that can help their peers move forward. | E1. Co-creating criteria sentence stems and cues for effective feedback, (i.e. summarizing "so what I'm hearing you say is...", questioning "When you said that, were you meaning...?") with their students to demonstrate active listening. | T1. Require students to take, build and reflect upon others' perspectives or ideas (IE/<u>Circle of Viewpoints</u>-style activities/ assessments) | L1. Design and model protocols for staff meetings and **professional** learning days that allow educators to build and reflect upon others' perspectives and ideas that educators can use in their classrooms. |

159

| At our school, you will see each of us 'Carrying the Banner' when... | | | |
|---|---|---|---|
| Our Students are... | Our Educators are... | Our Tasks... | Our Leaders... |
| S2. Taking and fulfilling roles, describing why their role is important and the roles that others play to complete a task/get the job done. | E2. Co-creating and modeling protocols to help students determine the skills, roles and division of work needed to complete different classroom tasks. | T2. Require students to determine what's needed to complete tasks and take and fulfill their role on a team. | L2. Model the use of staff strengths and talents to build working groups and take roles to solve classroom, team and school-wide challenges. |

| At our school, you will see each of us 'Carrying the Banner' when... | | | |
|---|---|---|---|
| Our Students are... | Our Educators are... | Our Tasks... | Our Leaders... |
| S3. Describing their strengths, the strengths of their peers and how they work together to solve a problem. | E3. Using, modeling and co-creating techniques with their students to find their strengths and the strengths of those around us (i.e. conferencing, talking circles, skills/interest inventories). | T3. Require students to demonstrate and reflect upon different skills and talents to be completed (i.e. Team-based learning, group problem solving). | L3. Co-create and model regular reflection protocols and structures that allow educators to reflect upon and share the impact of their work in solving different challenges. |

## MERCHANT OF HOPE

Believe that everyone wants to be great. No student, parent, or staff member wants to be a failure. However, there will be times when people lose their way. **Believe that you can inspire others** to be more and do more than they ever thought possible.

| At our school, you will see each of us being 'Merchants of Hope' when… | | | |
|---|---|---|---|
| **Our Students are…** | **Our Educators are…** | **Our Tasks…** | **Our Leaders are…** |
| S1. Sharing new ideas and taking on leadership roles to create a positive classroom/ school environment. | E1. Conferencing with students to learn about their ideas/ dreams and breaking them into smaller, manageable steps | T1. Are authentic classroom, school and community-based challenges that empower students to take and fulfill leadership roles. | L1. Conferencing with staff to determine their professional goals and breaking them into smaller, manageable steps. |
| S2. Supporting and encouraging their peers to meet their goals. | E2. Co-creating common language and protocols for students to give, receive and use feedback about short-term and long-term goals that matter to them. | T2. Require students to work collaboratively to establish common objectives and checkpoints to ensure the success of group projects and individual goals. | L2. Co-creating structures (learning partners, documentation protocols) and progress markers with staff to enable individuals and teams to meet their professional goals. |

| At our school, you will see each of us being 'Merchants of Hope' when… | | | |
| --- | --- | --- | --- |
| Our Students are… | Our Educators are… | Our Tasks… | Our Leaders are… |
| S3. Showing persistence by making multiple attempts and using multiple strategies to complete tasks, even when faced with challenges or setbacks. | E3. Providing varied supports and modeling structures for discussion and self-reflection to determine supports that are working and not working. | T3. Build resilience by requiring students to follow multiple steps, to use different tools/ skills, and to reflect on progress to be completed. | L3. Modeling reflection protocols and providing frequent opportunities for staff to stop, reflect, share and celebrate their progress with others. |

# About the Authors

Jimmy Casas has been an educator for over thirty years, serving twenty-two years as a school leader, including fourteen years as Principal at Bettendorf High School. Under his leadership, Bettendorf was named one of the Best High Schools in the country three times by Newsweek and US News & World Report.

Jimmy was named the 2012 Iowa Secondary Principal of the Year and was selected as runner-up NASSP 2013 National Secondary Principal of the Year. In 2014, Jimmy was invited to the White House to speak on the Future Ready Schools pledge. Jimmy is also the author of nine books, including the best-selling books *Culturize, Live Your Excellence, Handle with Care, and Recalibrate the Culture.* Jimmy is the owner and CEO of J Casas & Associates, where he serves as a professional leadership coach for school leaders across the country. Connect with Jimmy at: jimmycasas.com

Cale Birk is a former Head of Innovation from British Columbia, Canada and Imagineer and co-author of *Navigating Leadership Drift, PLC 2.0 - Collaborating for Impact in Today's Schools, The PLC 2.0 Toolkit, Changing Change Using Learner-Centered Design* and now his latest work, *Words on the Wall - Culturizing Your Classroom For Observable Impact* with Jimmy Casas.

An educator and high school principal in the public school system for more than 25 years, Cale's school was named one of the first model PLC schools in Canada after increasing student success rates across all grades and subject areas for five consecutive years. As Head of Innovation, Cale developed the Observable Impact Model that districts and schools across North America now use to answer the question, "What is our observable impact?" – the observable changes in practice that make the difference for all learners. Using the lens of "impact" rather than "action", Cale has helped district leaders, school leaders and teachers reimagine and implement strategic plans, school plans and collaborative team plans that have a direct 'line of sight' to where it matters the most—in classrooms with students and teachers.

In addition to his work as an author and facilitator, Cale is a TED talker and has been the keynote/featured speaker at national conferences and workshops in Canada, the United States, Asia, New Zealand and Australia. Connect with Cale at: birklearns@gmail.com, www.birklearns.com, @birklearns (X, Instagram), or Cale Birk (LinkedIn).

# More from ConnectEDD Publishing

Since 2015, ConnectEDD has worked to transform education by empowering educators to become better-equipped to teach, learn, and lead. What started as a small company designed to provide professional learning events for educators has grown to include a variety of services to help educators and administrators address essential challenges. ConnectEDD offers instructional and leadership coaching, professional development workshops focusing on a variety of educational topics, a roster of nationally recognized educator associates who possess hands-on knowledge and experience, educational conferences custom-designed to meet the specific needs of schools, districts, and state/national organizations, and ongoing, personalized support, both virtually and onsite. In 2020, ConnectEDD expanded to include publishing services designed to provide busy educators with books and resources consisting of practical information on a wide variety of teaching, learning, and leadership topics. Please visit us online at connecteddpublishing.com or contact us at: info@connecteddpublishing.com

## Recent Publications:

*Live Your Excellence: Action Guide* by Jimmy Casas

*Culturize: Action Guide* by Jimmy Casas

*Daily Inspiration for Educators: Positive Thoughts for Every Day of the Year* by Jimmy Casas

*Eyes on Culture: Multiply Excellence in Your School* by Emily Paschall

*Pause. Breathe. Flourish. Living Your Best Life as an Educator* by William D. Parker

*L.E.A.R.N.E.R. Finding the True, Good, and Beautiful in Education* by Marita Diffenbaugh

*Educator Reflection Tips Volume II: Refining Our Practice* by Jami Fowler-White

*Handle With Care: Managing Difficult Situations in Schools with Dignity and Respect* by Jimmy Casas and Joy Kelly

*Disruptive Thinking: Preparing Learners for Their Future* by Eric Sheninger

*Permission to be Great: Increasing Engagement in Your School* by Dan Butler

*Daily Inspiration for Educators: Positive Thoughts for Every Day of the Year, Volume II* by Jimmy Casas

*The 6 Literacy Levers: Creating a Community of Readers* by Brad Gustafson

*The Educator's ATLAS: Your Roadmap to Engagement* by Weston Kieschnick

*In This Season: Words for the Heart* by Todd Nesloney, LaNesha Tabb, Tanner Olson, and Alice Lee

*Leading with a Humble Heart: A 40-Day Devotional for Leaders* by Zac Bauermaster

*Recalibrate the Culture: Our Why...Our Work...Our Values* by Jimmy Casas

*Creating Curious Classrooms: The Beauty of Questions* by Emma Chiappetta

*Crafting the Culture: 45 Reflections on What Matters Most* by Joe Sanfelippo and Jeffrey Zoul

*Improving School Mental Health: The Thriving School Community Solution* by Charle Peck and Dr. Cameron Caswell

*Building Authenticity: A Blueprint for the Leader Inside You* by Todd Nesloney and Tyler Cook

*Connecting Through Conversation: A Playbook for Talking with Kids* by Erika Bare and Tiffany Burns

*The Dream Factory: Designing a Purposeful Life* by Mark Trumbo

*Stories Behind Stances: Creating Empathy Through Hearing "The Other Side"* by Chris Singleton

*Happy Eyes: Becoming All Things to All People* by Ryan Tillman

*The Generative Age Artificial Intelligence and the Future of Education* by Alana Winnick

*Recalibrate the Culture: Action Guide* by Jimmy Casas

*Leading with PEOPLE: A Six Pillar Framework for Fruitful Leadership* by Zac Bauermaster

*A School Leader's Guide to Reclaiming Purpose* by Frederick C. Buskey

*Foundations of an Elite Culture: Building Success with High Standards and a Positive Environment* by David Arencibia

*Personalize: Meeting the Needs of All Learners* by Eric Sheninger and Nicki Slaugh

*The Five Principles of Educator Professionalism: Rebuilding Trust in Schools* by Nason Lollar

# ConnectEDD
## PUBLISHING

www.ingramcontent.com/pod-product-compliance
Lightning Source LLC
Chambersburg PA
CBHW070111030426
42335CB00016B/2106